The Demarchy Manifesto

For Better Public Policy

John Burnheim

SOCIETAS
essays in political
& cultural criticism

imprint-academic.com

Published in the UK by
Imprint Academic, PO Box 200, Exeter EX5 5YX, UK

Distributed in the USA by
Ingram Book Company,
One Ingram Blvd., La Vergne, TN 37086, USA

ISBN 9781845408916

A CIP catalogue record for this book is available from the
British Library and US Library of Congress

For Luca Belgiorno-Nettis

You showed how to get things moving

The sickness of a time is cured by an alteration in the form of life of human beings, and it was possible for the sickness of philosophical problems to get cured only through a changed mode of thought and of life.

Ludwig Wittgenstein

Contents

Preface

The message of this book can be stated quite succinctly. We face problems that call for collective decision on matters of unprecedented importance and difficulty. If we are to have any chance of getting those decisions right, the procedures by which we come to them must be divorced from struggles for political power. There is a way of doing this that can be institutionalised without any exercise of power, just by voluntary organisations. I can't prove that my proposals will work, but I hope to convince enough people to give my suggestions a trial.

My views are based on a lifetime of academic study of all the various dimensions of the problem. If you spread your attention over so many fields your knowledge of most of them is going to be very thin. I can't claim to be an authority on any of them. The arguments in this book are put in simple language. Inevitably that involves a lot of over-simplification. What I ask of you, the reader, is that you make allowance for that, at least provisionally, until you can look at what I'm saying in a new perspective. The question I want you to ask is this: How do we get sound public policy?

Democratic theory and practice has been focused on problems of power. It is torn between two objectives, giving power to the people and minimising power over the individual. I accept that our present democratic institutions are a reasonable solution to most of those problems, but they are not a satisfactory way of getting sound policies on many matters. The focus has to be on what to do about that. I think that focus needs a new name. So I've tried to appropriate the word 'demarchy' for it.

The present text adopts an entirely different perspective from my *Is Democracy Possible?* That book was frankly utopian, speculating about the possibility of a complex of councils chosen by lot exercising all the functions of government. The present text is concerned with immediate practical problems. The time may come when the older text may take on a more practical relevance, if my present proposals are successful.

Over a very long lifetime I have acquired a host of debts to colleagues and friends with whom I have discussed the topics raised in this book. To do justice to those whom I should credit would call for a host of footnotes that my failing memory couldn't produce and readers could hardly assimilate. I confine myself to thanking those who have read and commented on various drafts of this book: Geoff Gallop, Paul Crittenden, Luca Belgiorno-Nettis, Creagh Cole, Denise Russell, Iain Walker, Keith Sutherland, Lyn Carson, Marcus Green, Elizabeth Johnston, Catherine Burnheim, Gavan Butler and Margaret Harris. I'm indebted to each of them for significant improvements to earlier drafts, as well as for their encouragement.

My editor, Kate Manton, helped turn a rambling mess into something more presentable. Thank you Kate.

To Margaret Harris I owe, beside her careful checking of the text, the fundamental gift of having kept me in excellent health and spirits into advanced old age.

John Burnheim
Sydney
September 20, 2015

Introduction

What I call 'demarchy' is primarily a process of transferring the initiative in formulating policy options from political parties to councils representative of the people most directly affected by those policies. The task of those councils would be to distil from public discussion the most acceptable policy in a particular matter. It would be up to voters to insist that the politicians heed them. There is no question of constitutional change, no new parties or new laws, no call for a mass conversion of opinion, but a suggestion about how to initiate a change in accepted practice, starting with actions that may seem of little significance in the big picture, but are still justified by their specific purposes. My focus is on how policy is produced and adopted. I am not concerned with questions about the philosophical basis of state power, or human rights, or crime and punishment. The precise forms these things take in practice are a matter of conventions, which I do not propose to challenge. There is already much debate about these matters. I am concerned about what I see as a more important, but neglected, question.

I begin by concentrating on how to establish some new practices and initiatives in policy formation, empowering those most affected to take the initiative in formulating what they want. It is no advantage to have a choice of products if none of those on offer meets your requirements. The best situation is to be able to say exactly what you want and commission specialists to supply it. Or is that analogy anachronistic and inappropriate in the era of mass production and distribution? I try to analyse our unique problems. My ultimate aim is to transform our political culture. I intend to show how different practices of policy formation are appropriate to different problems at every level from the local to the global and how they might come to be accepted.

Changing the paradigm

I am attempting to do three things:

- Show how to improve policy formation in government at the local and national levels, using procedures that confront politicians with an authoritative expression of what informed public opinion believes needs to be done in specific policy matters. The aim is to constrain politicians to legislate and administer in accordance with those policies.
- Propose that similar procedures could be used in establishing specialised global authorities strong enough to constrain national governments to conform to their decisions without anything like a world state.
- Suggest that we need to change some of the assumptions underlying much of our political thinking and practice in the light of the global ramifications of so many of our activities.

A central idea is to change the model of political communities that has dominated traditional thinking and practice. Political communities, typically nation-states, have been *personified* and taken as complete in themselves. All the diverse components should act in unison under the direction of the head, the brain. In a top-down sequence the design of the society is decided by a single authority and the other elements of the whole are forced to conform. In a constitutional state what the head is entitled to do is limited. Democracy also gives people a say in choosing those who exercise supreme authority. Each state is entirely independent of all the others. Relations between them can only be regulated by mutual agreement. There is no authority with the power to alter or enforce the set of conventions that constitute international law. On occasion groups of nations agree to punish other nations for what they see as breaches of international law, but they have no institutional authority to do so.

In early-modern times, when nation-states were largely homogeneous and self-sufficient, the model of the community as a person had a certain plausibility. I want to suggest that in the contemporary world it is obsolete and misleading. Instead, I suggest, the appropriate model of our situation is that of a global ecosystem consisting of a host of diverse subsystems, each with its specific needs and activities. Each of these subsystems has its relative independence from and interconnections with other systems. The order of any such whole arises from the interactions of its diverse constituents.

From an economic perspective we live in a world of international markets in all the most important commodities, of global communications, internationalised lifestyles and of moral concern about the rights of people all over the world. Freedom of trade, communications, lifestyles and action on human rights all depend on explicit and enforceable arrangements. At present we have no very satisfactory way of setting up such arrangements. In particular, we have developed physical and social technologies that change the processes on which all our ecosystems depend. Many of the activities we invent have systemic effects that can be very destructive. Those effects must be identified and controlled if the ecosystem we depend on is to survive and flourish. Our modern forms of life are oriented towards discovering more things to do individually and collectively. In many ways the social ecosystem is even more complex than its biological substrate. So the world we live in is changing rapidly, inevitably creating new problems or posing old ones on a new scale. It is essential that we develop flexible and effective ways of responding to these problems. What I am trying to get people to do is to look at my proposals in the light of that need, not just in terms of our habitual assumptions and aspirations.

Generating policy

People have become increasingly aware that the existing political processes cannot be relied on to produce sound decisions about matters of public policy.

What is wrong with politics? Many things: reliance on expensive and misleading advertising to sell package deals to the electorate; the power that gives to the media and to big money; the adversarial party system which limits and distorts people's choices, and so on. But the basic one is that many important matters are decided, not on the specific merits of the case, but according to the strategies of professional politicians seeking to maximise their power. Whether the politicians are motivated by a desire to serve their constituents or some philosophical ideal, as politicians they have to win the contest for power. I shall return to this problem in more detail later.

In both the struggle to attract key sections of the voters and the struggles for power within parties and coalitions, poor decisions are made and entrenched. Politicians are driven to make rash promises, to play on imaginary hopes and fears and to misrepresent the issues. There is much talk of accountability, but that usually reduces to getting politicians to make very specific promises and trying to hold them to fulfilling their undertakings. As the saying goes, sometimes the problem is that politicians break their promises, but often the problem is that they keep them. In the struggle for power in the legislature, politicians have to make deals for support in which they undertake to support measures and politicians they don't like in return for those others giving them support that would not otherwise be forthcoming on other matters that are usually irrelevant to that issue. To assure that particular policy proposals are assessed on their specific merits rather than on their tactical advantages we have to find ways of disentangling them from the struggle for power.

The political process has four stages or aspects: policy formation, legislation, execution and judicial enforcement. At present policy formation is in the hands of political parties, which, by a very poor set of decision procedures, attempt to present themselves as preferable to any of the other contestants. The electors are faced with a take-it-or-leave-it choice of packages that entrust the parties with many blank cheques. What my proposals aim to do is unscramble the packages and give people an effective say in policy formation, especially in matters that affect them directly. Public discussion of specific issues will be effective to the extent that it focuses on considerations directly relevant to those issues. By entrusting the task of formulating best policy on each issue to a distinct group of people who form a representative sample of the various people most directly affected by the outcome, we can ensure that no proposal is adopted for reasons that are irrelevant to its merits. On the other hand, any authority these decisions might claim would not rest on any formal status, but simply on their being seen as the best decisions available.

What I envisage is that the parties seeking election to legislative and executive office would present themselves to voters, not on the basis of promises or ideologies or sectional interests, but as willing and able to implement the policies that emerge from a sound decision process. At least the most important policy decisions would be made by the people, not the politicians. Instead of the public being offered whatever choices the politicians give them, the public now can make specific proposals and challenge the politicians to implement them. That should put an end to the cult of the leader as the guarantor of public policy. Creative leadership is needed in every activity, but it cannot be monopolized by a single person.

A new perspective

What I suggest, then, is that 'we' (just relatively small groups of people like you and me) can, if we so desire, initiate a revolution in the way our communities make decisions about public policy and public goods and services at every level, from the very local to the global, without a revolution in the classical sense of seizing state power and reforming things from the top down. Instead I argue that it is not just possible but necessary that we start from very specific problems and approach them in a new perspective, making much more use of practices that are already in use in limited contexts. Getting started does not presuppose any legislative change or official authorisation or even general agreement. The aim is to win recognition, not assume it. We have to support bodies that stimulate sound discussion and are capable of producing good, practical policy decisions.

The change of perspective I want to persuade you to adopt is as follows. Set aside for the moment the democratic obsession with giving everybody a vote on every matter that could possibly affect them, however little they know or care about it. Set aside visions of national self-sufficiency. Concentrate instead on how to get the best practical decisions on the very diverse matters where it is advantageous to make collective decisions. I am *not* saying: leave it to the experts, especially the producers. What I advocate is putting specific areas of policy in the hands of councils that are representative of those who are most substantially affected by those decisions, the key stakeholders in those matters, and getting them to coordinate their decisions with other councils by negotiation rather than direction from above. The point is to develop the ecosystem by ensuring the flourishing of its diverse constituents rather than to fit them into some preconceived design.

Present political practice acknowledges the fundamental importance of public opinion, as well as of expert opinion. Effective social policy has to be endorsed and valued by the community generally. Politicians are driven by polling and tie themselves in knots attempting to put an attractive spin on the policies they advocate, while their opponents attempt to vilify them. Public discussion is too often dominated by such adventitious factors. The results of answers to poll questions at best reflect what people see as particularly salient, not some balanced and informed discussion of the question. What we lack is a sound process of discussion and decision that is directed by concern about specific problems, enlightening public opinion about them, attempting to get beyond uncritical assumptions and ideologies. Bodies that can do that will have an authority that present forms of 'consultation', as well as partisan think-tanks and lobby groups, lack. The attitude that needs to dominate discussion and decision is that we are faced with a situation of diverse and often conflicting considerations, needing to find a practical, generally acceptable, solution to the problems of doing something constructive about them. Not everybody is going to agree with that solution, but nearly everybody will be prepared to accept it as the best we can do at the moment and look forward to reviewing its performance in due course.

My strategy is strictly practical. All that is required to get enough politicians to take notice of any proposed solution to a particular problem is that most uncommitted voters are in favour of it. The 'rusted-on' party faithful will tag along, once they recognise that accepting the proposal in question is preferable to losing power. It is not even necessary that most swing voters be convinced of the merits of my overall proposals. If they see the merits of the solutions that the councils devise to a number of important questions, they will gradually come to see those procedures as the best way of bypassing the partisan politics dominated by the struggle for power. The crucial task is to get a number of such councils up and running, each addressing some specific problem, independently of political parties and vested interests. They need to be adequately designed and funded so that they get the chance to prove themselves. I need to persuade enough people with the necessary resources to devote to that task.

I expect that the existence of impartial councils will have a salutary effect on public discussion. Interest groups in urging their cases will not concentrate on defeating their adversaries, but on reaching some acceptable compromise with them. They should try to influence the bodies that are working to evolve such compromises rather than relying on politicians to favour them over their adversaries. Power struggles will go on as long as there are institutions that operate by bloc voting, but those procedures will become increasingly irrelevant to the substance of our decisions and the perspectives in which we frame them.

I shall delay discussion of objections to my proposals until the third part of this text. For example, an obvious danger is that the orientation towards consensus favours feeble compromises at the expense of bold and incisive policies. My hope would be that concentrating discussion on very specific problems would minimise the effect of vague and familiar conceptions that often obscure more relevant considerations. If concentration on specific policies is seen as an experimental procedure, a process of collective learning by trial and error, policy-makers should be encouraged to try bold approaches where politicians are inclined to play it safe.

We live in an extremely complex network of interactions between various agencies. Our overriding common interest is that each and every one of the various operations involved in this global order should function as well as possible. Think of that order as an ecosystem, not a machine. Machines are designed for a purpose to which each part is wholly subordinate. Ecosystems are immeasurably more complex and have no overriding purpose. We are both part of a global ecosystem that adapts by natural selection to changing circumstances and also part of a social complex that operates by a mixture of design and unconscious interactions that often subvert design. We cannot avoid doing things that constitute making collective choices that have important effects. The ecosystem depends on biodiversity. Where we have to intervene is when our actions threaten that diversity. We also have the option of introducing new 'genes' into old contexts. Where the ecosystem analogy falls down is that we do not have to rely on natural selection or accept the catastrophic extinctions it can produce. We cannot control any large biosystem in the way we control machines, but we can, within limits, intervene to maintain the health of our biological ecosystems and improve the sustainability of our farms and gardens within them. Similarly, we can maintain the healthy growth of our social systems, our communities and networks, not by centralised planning, but by tackling specific problems on a scale and by methods that are appropriate to each case.

The shape of this text

I begin with some general considerations that seem relevant to understanding the presuppositions on which my proposals are based. The focus is on what various kinds of authorities can do, particularly in view of the limitations of their means of making sound decisions and implementing them. That leads me to suggest that in many contexts we need to develop new procedures, better adapted to specific problems. I try to characterise the procedures I have in mind in general terms and suggest some examples of how we might go about applying them to deal with some urgent problems. I conclude with answers to objections and some reflections on my hopes. My views are intended to be assessed pragmatically as proposals, not as theories that are supposed to cover all possibilities. They are calls for experimentation, not ideological commitment.

I am striving to get people to understand my proposals against a broad background with many dimensions, in the hope that they will be seen neither as just tinkering with our problems nor as a utopian dream. On the one hand, I want to insist on the importance of paying close attention to specific problems and starting from them. On the other, I want to suggest that the sort of approach I advocate can offer the hope of a new political order, a hope that may stimulate people to think and motivate them to act. This is most important, because the initiative has to come not from politicians but from popular movements inspired by a vision of a better political order. When politicians propose citizen juries to reach a consensus on some matter, they are usually seen as attempting to evade difficult decisions or construct a bogus endorsement for their own policies. So I am addressing neither politicians nor political theorists but people who are actively concerned with getting beyond our present situation. I want to get them thinking about how public opinion can be developed and made more effective as the driving force of a diversified polity.

The second part, outlining some specific suggestions, can be read on its own, but I fear that these suggestions may be dismissed as hopelessly vague. In fact, as I see it, all one can offer at this level of discussion is necessarily vague. Effective suggestions have to originate from within a particular practical context. Even the first and the third part can be read selectively, since they consist of remarks on distinct topics. But I hope you will take in the whole picture and be stimulated by the prospect.

The core ideas in this book were presented thirty years ago as an exercise in political theory,[1] attempting to explore what might be possible. Other political theorists declined to pursue the questions it sought to raise. It was all too utopian. A perceptive reviewer said it would have been much better to present them as practical proposals. I have been encouraged by increasing interest in these and closely related suggestions[2] to follow his advice, rather belatedly.

What follows is sketchy. It does not aim to prove anything. It is directed towards getting people to test my proposals in practice. I have used the word 'demarchy' to label my pro-posals. 'Demarchy' was used centuries ago in much the same pejorative way as 'anarchy'. F.A. Hayek attempted, without success, to appropriate it for his political proposals, which never gained much traction, even among his disciples. I attempted to steal it from him, again with limited success. And other people have attempted to steal it from me. I am making another attempt to grab it back. In wars over words usage decides. I would be happiest, however, if the word came into general use to mark the difference between democratic regimes focused on power and sovereignty and regimes focused on sound decision-making. That might restore the term to the broad sense that Hayek had in mind, of supplanting many of

---

[1] *Is Democracy Possible? The alternative to electoral politics.* By John Burnheim. Cambridge, Polity Press; Berkeley, University of California Press, 1985. 2nd ed. Sydney University Press, 2006; setis.library.sydney.edu.au/democracy. Kindle edition on Amazon.

[2] The Sydney-based New Democracy Foundation has attracted a wide range of support, especially from politicians and academics. For international developments see the appendix at the end of this text.

the defective procedures of populist democracy while remaining faithful to the concerns for people's freedom and well-being that have inspired it.

The essential change is to minimise power politics, symbolised by the suffix 'cracy' in such words as 'autocracy' and 'democracy' and in slogans like 'power to the people'. I claim that what is wrong with populist democracy is the assumption that there is an entity, the 'people', usually identified as a particular race or historical group that can and should exercise ultimate decision power in all public matters that affect those who live in a certain territory, or belong to a certain historical group, or a certain religion, or a certain class. This leads to unsatisfactory structures and processes at the national level and to a disastrous failure to address our urgent global problems.

On traditional democratic assumptions what matters is the choice of those who exercise ultimate sovereignty on behalf of the people. Democracy is usually taken as demanding that the rulers be chosen by mass voting on a universal adult suffrage from candidates who belong to unified parties. This procedure has the unique merit of enabling the people to throw out a ruling team, which is certainly something that must be preserved. However, in the absence of other means of arriving at policy decisions, it also means that voters have to buy a package of policies, leading politicians to claim a 'mandate' to implement those policies, many of which people voted for only to get rid of the previous government. This has led to a growing backlash, an insistance that in voting for a party people are not giving it a blank cheque. Those most affected by specific policies need to be consulted before they are implemented. The ways in which this 'consultation' proceeds at the moment are very defective. There are better ways of achieving good policy decisions and getting them accepted.

Demarchy's ambitions

If demarchy is to become a practical movement, not just a theoretical speculation, it is bound, like the regimes it strives to replace, to appeal to different people for different reasons, particularly in view of what they see as the key deficiencies in democracy as we know it. Opinions will differ about what is desirable or at least worth trying. Among the desired changes I hope will emerge are the following transitions:

- From bundling together different issues to distinguishing the specific considerations and constituencies most relevant to each.
- From looking at particular issues as weapons in a struggle for power to judging them on their merits.
- From according absolute supremacy to national sovereignty to treating global issues in a global perspective and communities within the nation in the light of their particular needs.
- From seeing the public interest as a totality to seeing it as a complex of many overlapping mini-publics, each based on different kinds of interactions and areas of decision.
- From the illusion that there is such a thing as 'the will of the people' to the realisation that we all have, even within ourselves, conflicting interests between which we need to negotiate practical compromises.
- From the idea that we each have a single identity and set of interests to seeing ourselves as having multiple interests and connections of different sorts.
- From glorifying or just accepting zero-sum or even lose-lose games to constructing win-win ones.
- From emphasis on 'freedom from' to 'freedom to'.
- From fear of organisation as potentially tyrannical to designing particular limited organisations as suited to doing specific things that need to be done.
- From aspirations to construct the sort of society we want by centralised top-down action to seeing society as built from the bottom up by appropriate decisions in a host of different activities.
- From elections by mass voting to sortition (selection by lot), as the characteristic means of citizen representation in policy-making bodies.

- From seeing a society as a single organism to seeing it as a continually evolving ecosystem, resulting from the activities of a host of different interdependent but unplanned organisms and processes.

As will become apparent, I think all of these transitions, and many others, are both desirable and possible, but this is not a package that has to be accepted or rejected as a whole. What demarchy proposes is a revolutionary change in the way we make decisions about public goods without a revolutionary mobilisation of power. It is a constructive process of introducing and testing better ways of public decision-making. Our perspectives and problems are bound to change in the process.

That, you may say, is a list of vague hopes. If this is a manifesto, it should be a call to action. So what do you want us to do? And how are we supposed to do it?

1. Set up a public foundation, financed by voluntary contributions, run by an executive that inspires trust, completely divorced from any political party or commercial interest. Its sole objective is to promote discussion of public policy issues.

2. The foundation identifies a particular policy issue that requires discussion and formulates it as a practical problem that needs attention.

3. The foundation announces its intention to invite public submissions from any source on what needs to be done, and promises that they will be carefully and publicly debated by a select council with a view to getting a clear conclusion about what needs to be done.

4. At the same time it invites people who are interested in serving on that council to volunteer to join a panel from which the membership of the council will be selected by lot within certain categories, reflecting the different ways in which ordinary people are most strongly and directly affected by policy in the matter under discussion. The panel must accept this arrangement almost unanimously.

5. It is made clear to the members of the council that they are there to comment publicly on and adjudicate between the

various considerations raised in public discussion. They are not there as representatives of whatever interest they have in the outcome. Usually most of the proposals put up for discussion will come from experts. A large part of the role of council members in the discussion is to make sure that what the experts and amateur theorists propose is acceptable to those who have to bear the consequences of whatever is decided.

6. Neither the foundation, nor the panel, nor the council claims any right to speak on behalf of anybody else. The policy they decide on needs to be widely accepted as a fair conclusion from the public discussion for it to have any claim to authority. If the members of the council fail to get their work accepted on that basis they will just be wasting their time.

7. In the light of a general recognition of the need to deal with the problem, what the council decides may well be generally accepted as the best policy to follow in the circumstances, even by many who would prefer another approach. That attitude should become prevalent if such decisions are subsequently implemented and turn out well.

8. Faced with a clear expression of public opinion the government would be under very strong pressure to implement the council's policy. Politicians would compete as efficient managers of public business, rather than as constructing policy packages.

9. If this process gave good results in practice, it should become accepted as best practice in arriving at policy decisions and continually be refined and developed in the light of experience. It should result in divorcing discussion of public policy from struggles for power, educate public opinion, and produce increasingly better outcomes.

Part One

Exploring the Problems

Decisions

Freedom comes in two guises: freedom of spontaneity, which is always delightful, and freedom of choice, which is frequently onerous, particularly when much is at stake and we can't avoid making a choice. Some actions, or even omissions, constitute making a decision, even though we are not conscious of making any decision. We simply act out of habit or instinctive reaction. Our action is said to constitute a decision because it can be seen as committing us to a particular set of results, which would not have been the case if we had chosen some other course of action. As we become more aware of the ways in which we commit ourselves to one set of outcomes rather than another we become more aware of choosing as imposed upon us. Working out the various consequences of different choices is often complicated and difficult. It may not be worth the trouble, perhaps because the chances of our getting the consequences right are no better than chance or because the differences between the options are unimportant. We might as well toss a coin.

Many people feel that way about even quite important decisions. They regard making decisions in most contexts not as an advantage but a burden. Such an attitude can take many forms, ranging from the monk who discards choice in nearly all the affairs of life to devote himself to higher things under strict discipline, to the frivolous who finds seriousness about most choices ridiculous. Both have a point as opposed to the person who treats every decision with equal seriousness. We have to economise our use of time and energy if we are to concentrate on the things that matter most to us. In many matters we simply follow normal routines of behaviour. In others we follow the example or advice of others who are in a better position than we are to assess the choices available to us. Increasingly we have recourse to decision tools such as budgeting to maximise the utility we get from our income or taking out insurance against potential disasters. For some of us such calculated choices give us the agreeable feeling that our lives are under our own control. For others they represent the loss of spontaneity.

When it comes to collective decisions, similar considerations apply. We live in an extremely complex society in which many alternative decision tools are available to us. We are faced with the problem of which tools to use and how much attention we ought sensibly to devote to the various choices to be made. There is no way in which most of us can be well informed about most of those choices. We have to trust others who are in a better position to make sound decisions to decide on our behalf. In traditional monarchies and aristocracies it was assumed that ordinary people lacked the ability and the information necessary to make political decisions. They had to trust those who inherited that capacity. In modern conceptions of democracy inherited privilege was overthrown and ordinary people were allowed to choose those who were to make decisions on their behalf. The development of modern democracy has been in the direction of making the politicians more responsive to public opinion, but we have a long way to go to get to the end of that road.

Representative government saw the conduct of government as properly directed to the ordinary interests of the citizens, not to any superior end, as many older regimes, especially those devoted to a religion, assumed. That raised the question of what was the appropriate means of choosing those who managed the affairs of the people. Many harked back to ancient Athens, where all questions of public policy were decided at meetings in which every citizen could participate directly, while the administrative tasks were delegated to smaller bodies chosen by lot as (in the case of the Council of 500) a representative sample of the citizens. Modern advocates of direct participation in policy decisions often saw referendums on policy issues as a practical modern equivalent of the Athenian assembly. Others saw choosing by lot those who formulated and legislated public policy in our parliamentary institutions as a better solution. Aristotle, one of the greatest of political theorists, criticised decision-making by mass voting in the *ecclesia* as leading to rule by the orators who swayed the voters by rhetoric rather than sound argument. The corresponding criticism of proposals for mass voting on all major policy issues is that it gives too much sway to the mass media. I shall return to these questions shortly.

My own proposals take a different view of representation. It is indeed important that the decisions on matters that affect the interests of ordinary people be taken by people who are representative of those particular interests. They are normally the best judges of what is good for them, provided they are well informed about the consequences of the options open to them and are motivated to devote the time and energy necessary for a thorough deliberation about the alternatives. Many public policy matters nowadays admit of many variants. More importantly still, many conflicting considerations are involved in assessing those variants. The best way of resolving the conflict between such different considerations is by discussion of possible compromises and negotiation among those who are differently affected by these considerations. Resources are always limited. Not everything that is desirable is equally possible or equally desirable. Experience of debate on citizen committees on public policy shows that people frequently change their view about the best option in the light of discussion and negotiation with those who are equally involved in the problem, but have somewhat different experiences, preferences and preconceptions. If those involved in making the decision see their task not as doing whatever it takes to get what best suits them, but as getting the best solution to a shared problem, the result is likely to be accepted by all those affected as the best that can be achieved in the circumstances.

Take, for example, a regional health service. A policy issue that is very likely to arise is how much certain specialist facilities are to be spread over a number of centres in the region and how much they are to be concentrated in a single centre. On the one hand spreading them makes access to them much easier for most people, while on the other concentrating them ensures much more efficient use of staff and equipment and considerable savings in other respects. It is very unlikely that the best answer to this problem is a blanket policy of either centralisation or decentralisation. It may be difficult to afford a full range of specialists in a certain locality, but it may be possible to provide some sophisticated machine that sends results to a specialist who can read them in some central location as easily as if she were on the spot. There is an enormous difference between top-down policy decisions between pre-set alternatives and serious confrontation with the different costs and benefits that policies have in different situations. There is a tension between different conceptions of fairness. On the one hand it may seem to demand uniformity of results for everybody, so that those with greater need receive more resources, while others may emphasise equal entitlements for each person where there is a question of rationing scarce resources and not all needs can be met.

There is another set of considerations that are relevant to both individual and personal decisions besides those of maximising quantifiable benefits and minimising costs, namely those that are called expressive. They apply to those aspects of our actions and decisions that are not just instrumental, done purely in order to achieve some goal, but are done because we like doing them, quite independently of anything else they produce. They are called expressive because they are usually attractive to us, since in performing them we express something about ourselves that we value. Or we avoid them because we wish to disavow what we take them to express. We like to appear generous, not mean, and so on with other moral and psychological attributes, including a devotion to things that we consider as worthy of our respect and concern, quite independently of any benefit those things may bring us personally. In practice the relations between the two types of considerations are very complicated. People often act in a way that expresses admirable qualities in order to ingratiate themselves with others. More generally, some qualities are considered admirable because they are socially useful. When it comes to collective decisions a community's conception of itself as manifested in certain kinds of behaviour is often a powerful reason for the choices it makes. Sometimes instrumental considerations are called rational, because they may admit of precise, objective calculation, as opposed to expressive considerations, which resist calculation and have an ineliminable subjective element. That is a very narrow conception of reason. We do argue rationally about the relevance of different qualities to different decisions.

What is politics about?

There is a cynical or, more euphemistcally, 'realist' view of politics that describes it as being about 'who gets what'. That is indeed how very many people have played it and still do, from the politics of dynasties wrangling over territory to modern politicians squabbling over zoning laws. Obviously many political decisions do affect who gets what, but that is not their basic function. What politics is about is the construction and preservation of public goods. What monarchs fighting over territory were supposed to be doing was defending the honour, security and prosperity of the realm. The point of zoning laws is to enable various kinds of activity to go on in an environment that is congenial to their different requirements. Good decisions on public policy are directed to good designs to sustain certain kinds of public goods. What we need as members of various communities are public goods that enhance our social lives. To achieve that we need decision-making bodies that are well equipped and strongly motivated to make good decisions on specific policy issues.

Getting sound decisions about public goods is dependent on finding ways of approaching the issues, not just in terms of their benefits to individual private interests but in their social role as common goods. In one way it is true that there is no such thing as society, as Margaret Thatcher pronounced. In the same sense there is no such thing as ice. The physicists assure us that all the properties of ice can be explained in terms of the properties of the molecules of H_2O, as can the properties of steam, clouds, snowflakes and water. There is no other ingredient that has to be added to the existing molecules to produce the particular properties of ice as distinct from the other forms its components can assume. The differences are entirely a matter of the configurations in which the molecules are organised. In ice they are regimented into a rigid pattern of balanced forces, which is highly stable within a certain temperature range. At the other extreme steam results from those molecules being disposed in an almost wholly random arrangement, which can mix with other gaseous fluids to form various kinds of vapour or with dust particles to form fog, and so on.

For most purposes we have to deal with H_2O in some specific form, not just as a collection of molecules. It is the properties of those particular forms that are relevant to our concerns and to the great variety of uses to which we can put them. Even a stray molecule of H_2O encountering a block of ice has to deal with the molecules it first encounters, not just as one-on-one, but as organised in a stable and mostly powerful organisation. If the temperature of the ice is well below freezing point, it will almost certainly be frozen on to the block. Similarly, we rarely encounter each other simply as random individuals, but almost always in some social role in which we are interconnected with many other people in quite specific ways. Those social relationships affect profoundly the nature and outcome of various encounters between people who, taken as isolated individuals, may be almost indistinguishable. We are tempted to ignore many of those relationships because they are not anything we can perceive directly in the way that we can see individual human beings or lumps of ice. But we know very well that both in nature and in social relationships many forms of organisation make a great deal of difference, even though we cannot see those differences with our limited sensory equipment.

This fact poses an enormous range of problems for us in our dealings with each other and with the ecosystems on which we depend for survival. We often like to be able to do whatever we happen to desire in the way that many animals do in the wild, but we cannot ignore the fact that we have so altered both nature itself and our relations to it and to each other that most of us could not possibly survive for more than a few days if the complex social mechanisms that supply us with the necessities of life were to break down completely. More positively, we have no possibility of turning back to a simpler form of life, say that of hunter-gatherers living in small groups. It is impossible to feed the present population of the world without science-guided agriculture and a great deal of trade in food over long distances. Paradoxically, this interdependence makes it easier for us to survive. Faced with severe drought many members of a hunter-gatherer group with limited ability to trade and no way of storing food would die of starvation. The growth of the population was limited. In our case continually developing agricultural technology combined with the control of most lethal diseases has greatly increased life expectancies and infant survival rates. But clearly our resources are limited and if population grows exponentially, many of us will be killed prematurely, as surely as hunter-gatherers in a severe drought.

The hope that population growth can be curbed naturally is that child bearing will become expensive for almost everybody and unattractive to many. We know that in our most prosperous communities rates of reproduction are barely sufficient to replace deaths, and that the main possibility of limiting population growth in poorer countries is to increase prosperity on the assumption that they will follow a similar pattern. It is possible for economic growth to happen very rapidly, but it is doubtful whether it is possible for all the newly rich to enjoy all the goods that form part of the lifestyle of most prosperous countries. There is probably no difficulty in everybody in the world having a mobile phone and a television set, but probably not a motorcar.

The first point I wish to make with this example is that many decisions on such matters as free trade and investment in poor countries are connected with the crucial problem of population and the limits of our resources. We have to attempt to make and implement decisions that will have the results we need to achieve. There is no guarantee that we can in fact deal effectively with our problems. Our efforts may make them worse, but we can be very sure that many potentially disastrous outcomes are inevitable, unless we succeed in doing something about them. The second point is that many problems cannot be dealt with by direct action, but only by tackling other problems effectively. One of the themes I wish to emphasise is that problems are best defined, analysed and discussed from a practical point of view when they are approached in terms of what is specific to them and what we can do about those specific matters.

What can we do?

Faced with the tremendous scale of the problems we have made for ourselves, a natural reaction is to think that we need a world government that can address our problems on a global scale deploying sweeping powers in the way that the governments of particular states do within their territories. That state would be conceived on the analogy of existing federal states, subject to democratic control and possessing only the very specific powers delegated to it in its constitution. I believe this view is mistaken, for reasons that relate particularly to what I see as a more adequate conception of authority and the diverse ways in which it can operate. That will emerge only gradually. It is true that there are certain problems that need to be tackled on a world scale, and that there is little hope of reaching satisfactory solutions to these problems by negotiation among existing states. What states do is determined by their internal politics. However, it is not always necessary for a specialised world authority to enjoy power to enforce its decisions in order to secure conformity to them. There are already many international authorities governing specific activities effectively without enjoying such power. So a world state may be unnecessary to do what needs to be done on many issues. My thesis is that if a competent specialised independent body devises a plan of action, powerful inducements from within and without will persuade states to do what is required by that plan. The politics of a world state operating the same decision procedures as nation states would be fatal to sound decisions.

For my thesis to work people have to be ready to see the decisions of a specialised supranational body not as an imposition on them, or a loss of control of their own affairs, but as a way of solving a shared problem analogous to the way that supranational aviation rules and procedures are universally accepted as ensuring safe coordination of air traffic. Such acceptance is easy when the issues are mainly technical, but very much more difficult where significant conflicts of interest are involved. If, as I suggest, such problems can be solved by public discussion and negotiation in a small representative group, and such procedures become widely accepted, it should be possible to get them accepted even in difficult cases where agreed action is clearly necessary. It is not necessary that such procedures become dominant in the political culture of nearly all nation states, but only that, under pressure, most are ready to go along with them in certain circumstances. The rule of law, as that is understood in most advanced countries, is not part of the culture of some others, but in certain international matters they submit to it. In many practical matters that is all that is required. People can be very ingenious in finding reasons to do what they have to do. Cultures are multi-stranded entities that can change very rapidly in particular respects without losing their identity.

The more specific and practical the problem for which action is required, the more likely it is to be possible to reach agreement on it, in spite of differences of interests and ideologies. Where a particular decision represents a practical compromise between conflicting considerations on a multi-dimensional problem, it is less likely to be seen as a matter of principle. Even if a group is opposed to it, believing that it rests on false assumptions, it may accept that the only way of getting beyond what they see as a poor decision is to allow it to be tried as an experiment in the hope that its deficiencies will become apparent in the outcome. We have to recognise that any concrete action is quite likely to have consequences that are different from those that its proponents expected. We make mistakes. What matters most is that we learn from our mistakes just where we went wrong and are open to suggestions of how to do better.

One of the impediments that our present political processes place in the way of such precisely focused pragmatic approaches to practical decisions is that they are directed towards presenting people with a choice between two comprehensive sets of policies, articulated in terms of particular promises. The voters are required to choose between these packages. In exercising that choice the electorate is supposed to take charge of the direction of public policy and of what is to be done about some specific matters of great interest to many of them. What is clear is that in practice it does not seem to work in the required way. Too often the contents of the packages and the spin that is put on them seem deceptive. I have already said something about two of the reasons why the packages put to voters are usually poorly constructed, namely that power trading among politicians leads to poor decisions and that key elements of the packages are intended to appeal to particular sections of the electorate to the neglect of other interests. This may seem inevitable if the citizens are to be faced with a straight choice, to be decided by counting votes. Is it the price we pay for having a choice of governments?

Voting and democracy

Voting is most appropriate where there is a clear choice between several alternatives that are appropriately defined – as when there is question of choosing the most suitable candidate for a position or where to go for a night out. The background assumption normally is that each of the alternatives in question is an acceptable choice. So in stable parliamentary democracies it is assumed that whichever party or coalition is chosen will perform the duties of governing in a way that is at least tolerable to the supporters of the opposition. Where the interests of the parties on matters of importance are mutually exclusive and there is a permanent majority in favour of one alternative, as in societies that are split into intolerant religious or racial sections, majority voting is no longer a viable way of choosing a government to produce common goods. Some kind of compromise that ensures that the minority has some say on matters that are important to it is necessary if the regime is to be acceptable to almost all of the citizens.

It is often said that the great virtue of electoral democracy is that it makes it easy for citizens to get rid of an unacceptable government by a peaceful procedure. However, the work of legislation and administration has to go on, and the practical possibility of throwing out an existing government depends on there being an acceptable alternative. In practice that means that there is a cohesive and competent group to which the task may be entrusted. That in turn works best when two opposing teams alternate from time to time, as one party is seen as having run out of fresh ideas or having become too compla-cent, while the other offers hope of new blood. Political parties are an important component of this process. Even though voters choose individuals to represent their particular constitu-ency, they usually choose between candidates mainly on party affiliation. They know that the member generally has a much better chance of advancing their particular interests through influence in a party than as a solitary member. They are also usually more concerned about the general tendency of the government than about any particular issue. It is the party that exercises power and bears the responsibility for the results.

Nevertheless, parties have notorious deficiencies, especially when they are split into factions. It is possible for a small minority to control a faction and for the faction to dominate the party, which in turn dominates the legislature and the administration. It is in this process that politics as a matter of who gets what comes into sharpest focus in the struggle of competing individuals and groups to maximise their power by trading favours. The mechanism is ubiquitous, in company boardrooms, bureaucracies and many other kinds of social organisations. When we bundle a large range of decisions on quite different matters together and charge the same group of people with producing acceptable decisions about each of those matters, they will often find themselves forced to rely on power trading to have any influence on the final decision. Most of those decisions call for compromises between conflicting considerations. People are bound to disagree about the relative weight given to those diverse considerations in particular instances. So the choice between the available alternatives is inevitably to some degree arbitrary and, because they affect different people substantially, highly contentious. So how can we reach an effective decision? If we bundle all those decisions together, what happens?

Suppose a lot of decisions are to be made by a group of people who are a fair sample of the population on whose behalf they make all those decisions. Suppose also that the decision on each matter is to be made by a simple majority of votes and that all do vote on every issue. For their differing reasons they each regard securing a particular result in respect of some particular issue as much more important than any particular result on many other issues. It will very often happen that on the issue they most care about a group of representatives will find themselves in a minority. What can they do to avoid defeat?

Their only recourse is to persuade a sufficient number of other representatives who don't share their view to vote for it in spite of not being inclined to do so. The obvious way of achieving that is to do a deal. One group (let's call them the As) contracts with another group (Bs) who can provide them with the votes they need. The deal is that the As vote with the Bs on some other issue the As care less about. The effect is that very many decisions are the result of such deals. The assembly adopts a proposal not because a majority thinks it is the best proposal, but because of the importance that some minority group that would not otherwise support it attaches to getting support in some very different connection. That is normally quite irrelevant to the merits of the proposal. The only way to get good decisions is to make sure that they are made on the basis of the relevant considerations. As we shall see, that is not always easy.

When power trading is generalised it leads to parties that concentrate power by organising representatives into complex deals on all the main issues. Parties draw lines in the sand and oblige everybody to jump to one side or the other and to commit themselves to a package deal. Of course, all the deals can't be tied up in advance. The situation is constantly changing and deals are being renegotiated within and between the parties. Some participants are much better than others at making deals. The less one cares about the issues the more flexibility one has in dealing. An unscrupulous LBJ, anxious to leave his mark on history, can be surprisingly effective. An Obama with a lot of commitments finds it much more difficult to strike a deal on anything. The process of dealing is open to corruption. Astute operators never lose an opportunity of putting those who might be useful to them in their debt. There are many economical ways of doing that, short of outright bribery and intimidation, as every lobbyist knows.

The result is inevitably a lot of sub-optimal decisions and a degree of tyranny. Each of us has to put up with many disadvantages because of decisions taken for the wrong reasons. Minorities rule. Robert Dahl, one of the great figures of American political thinking, recognised this, but argued that it doesn't matter as much as we might think, because it rarely results in very bad decisions, and the minorities are constantly changing. It may be more important to get something done than to wait until the best can be achieved. In mass voting where most of the voters can know little about the merits of the package of policies or the people that they are voting for, they can at least throw out a party that is manifestly failing to do what is needed. But that is no great consolation if the alternative is equally unpalatable. It is not a good system. But, as Churchill put it, aren't all the alternatives worse?

My key claim is that the change that is required is to separate the procedures by which we decide what policies to adopt from the procedures by which we choose those who implement them. In my view the present system works well enough as a way of choosing the executive of our governmental institutions. What is required of a good chief executive is the ability to organise support for particular tactical decisions, coordinate the workings of different branches of an organisation and communicate with those who need what it produces. To a large extent the qualities needed to succeed in power struggles within a political party are congruent with those that are required in the top executive role, to get things done and be seen to do so. The qualities required for making sound policy decisions are almost antithetical. In practical action short-term tactical considerations are trumps, while in policy matters what is important is to consider a comprehensive range of considerations and explore the possibility of diverse choices. Solving problems of policy often depends on considering different ways of looking at a situation. In implementing a decision, executives have to be able to command their subordinates to conform to their decisions, whatever their personal view of what is required. In formulating a common policy what is needed is open-ended discussion and persuasion to achieve unforced and sustainable agreement in a relatively longer-term perspective.

It is not surprising that in the most successful democracies emphasis has been placed on personalities rather than on policy. It has been assumed that the differences in policy between the parties were largely a matter of emphasis. The parties acknowledge the relevance of the same considerations, but put somewhat different relative weight on them. A balance was achieved over time by alternating them in office. What mattered most was effective and efficient conduct of the business of government. So the main ground on which many voters made their choice was the personality of the party leader, whether they would do the job well. Voters often had to make that choice on the basis of very superficial appearances, but they were entitled to assume that anybody who got to the top in the highly competitive struggles for power within a major party was likely to be at least reasonably competent.

In relatively simple, stable and homogeneous societies it was easy to assume that what nearly everybody needed from government was much the same. What one looked for in voting was good management of public affairs. Policy differences were relatively minor, such as whether to increase the old-age pension or to spend more money on education. While a pensioner voter would count it as a point in favour of a party that it promised to increase pensions, they would also recognise that assessing the effects that might have on other important public responsibilities had to be taken into account and it was the task of government to make those decisions prudently. People were vaguely aware both of the limits of their understanding of many of these matters and of the limits of the information that a vote could convey. Not only does a simple yes-no answer to a question have value only if it is appropriately phrased, but tallying the answers to arrive at a collective decision is a poor way of arriving at a decision on a matter of any complexity. It conveys no information about the reasons people have for giving more weight to one consideration rather than another. So it may well happen that there is a majority yes vote for a party based on the coincidence that several groups happen to have a weak preference for one or other of its policies, but a slightly smaller but united group is very strongly against that party because of some major interest that they all share.

If people were negotiating to produce the greatest good of the greatest number in terms of the strength of the preferences of the individuals involved they would have to give more weight to the strong preferences held by a large number than to the weak preferences of several smaller groups that chose to vote together. They would almost certainly arrive at a different decision on the basis of that information about the reasons for those votes than a decision based on merely counting votes. Indeed, recognising the complexity of these decisions, they might well agree with the view, famously put forward by Edmund Burke, that his commission was not to do the will of the voters, but to contribute to good governance. It was in accordance with a widespread acceptance of that view that most voters throughout the nineteenth century tended to elect those whom they saw as their betters. Voters were predominantly conservative, wary of the use of government to change society in either a reactionary or a progressive direction. The conservatives came to accept the welfare state when the failure of the market to deal with the Great Depression combined with experience of the success of government in mobilising resources for total war convinced people that government could deal effectively with many needs that the market could not satisfy. That confidence in the welfare state was in turn shaken as the resurgent market made available an unprecedented variety and quantity of novel goods and services while people came to see government bureaucracies as unresponsive and inefficient. Since then things have become very much more complicated and decisions more difficult.

In order to understand the problems of reaching decisions it is useful to look at all forms of organization—physical, biological and social—as information systems. Take the relationship between the sun's mass and the earth's mass. Left to itself the earth would travel in a straight line into outer space, but the sun's mass sends it signals which instruct it to change direction in complex ways, with the result that it orbits around the sun in a completely predictable pattern. Why talk of this relationship in terms of information? Because its functioning as an exchange of information is what enables us to understand it precisely. We can extract the structure of that information and express it completely in a set of interrelated symbols, mathematical equations, that we can manipulate according to precise rules to mimic any possible state of that relationship and indeed any possible relationship of one mass to another, at least within certain limits. Those limits are set by the fact that all the interchanges of information are dependent on the speed of light, and that happens to behave very strangely in extreme cases, as Einstein explained.

Of course, most of the information systems we encounter in our experience are very much more complex than gravitational attraction. In general, the more complex they are, the more difficult they are to model precisely. For the most part we have to settle for models that we know are oversimplifications of the signal exchanges that are going on. But they are better than nothing. They enable us to store and process — in neural patterns in our brains, in social constructs like money, in marks in books and bytes in computers — enormous amounts of more or less useful information. The difficulty it poses is that we can have only very unreliable information about the shortcomings of our information and how well it works in the roles in which we may want to cast it. That leaves room for a lot of disagreement about what models best fit what roles. But such disagreements are not necessarily fatal to communication. In practice we employ two diametrically opposed strategies for overcoming disagreement. One is to make our models more abstract, stripping them of information, in the hope that they will apply more generally to certain widely occurring patterns of information exchange, leaving aside other patterns that are also present in many particular cases. That approach is exemplified in social matters by economic theory, which models exchanges in so far as they are sensitive to market prices. The other approach is to seek to bring together a number of models that seem to exemplify most of the information exchanges in a certain concrete situation and attempt to see how they fit together. This approach is that of historical sociology, and, I believe is what is usually appropriate in practical decision-making, where we are attempting to get agreement about what to do in a particular situation by considering the relevance of a variety of considerations.

In general the abstraction approach works best when we have precise mathematical equations containing symbols that stand in for particular quantities and precise practical ways of assigning exact numbers to those quantities in a very wide range of circumstances. In the theory of mechanical interactions we have simple formulae and simple means of measuring length, mass and time. In economics the equations are less simple and money a less reliable metric, but nevertheless economic theory does explain many interactions. If I am right about practical political decisions needing to take the path of assembling as much diverse but relevant information as possible in order to arrive at a realistic decision in a specific matter, the question then is how to select what is relevant and how to interrelate the diverse models or information inter-changes they reveal. The short answer is to bring together people who are inclined to use different models and have them try to convince each other to concede something to each that constitutes a bridge of understanding and opens up the possibility of a decision that is as acceptable from those different points of view as possible. As I envisage such a process it is not primarily a matter of compromise but of mutual education as people come to see what others see in the situation and make due allowance for it. Obviously, it can never pretend to deliver as precise or certain a result as our best theories of single factors.

This model of information interchange clearly presupposes that the people in question can set aside adversarial relations in favour of maximum cooperation. But it does not suppose that they are bound to think of themselves as pure information processors. They can be strongly motivated to get the most generally accepted decision possible simply because their ability to persuade others to accept their conclusion will depend on having a solid claim to doing just that. Rationally, if they are strongly affected by what is done in the matter, they should acknowledge that it is likely to be in their interest to get such acceptance. Others will accept their decision, not so much because they see the participants as like themselves in most relevant respects, but because they trust the sort of decision procedure that is in use as appropriate to arriving at a sound decision. So they accept that any group acting on the same information would be likely to arrive at a similar decision.

For such a strategy to succeed it is vital that it is tried and proves satisfactory in practice. That involves a lot of organisation and resources, involving many active participants who understand and endorse the rationale of what they are expected to do. For their work to be accepted as what it purports to be does involve a broader change in political culture. We need to get away from ideologically 'holistic' approaches to our problems. Such approaches judge proposals primarily in terms of their expressive function, how they exemplify the concerns and aspirations that are seen as most desirable. Such considerations cannot and ought not be excluded from discussion, but in the context of practical problems the primary considerations must be those of practical effectiveness in dealing with those problems. Once we do that we can think of our political identity not along some single one-dimensional scale, but as involving a host of interconnections that constitute information exchanges, many of which we cannot understand at all adequately, much less control. The point of understanding what we are trying to deal with as an information system is that we stand a better chance of effective intervention to produce a desired outcome if we know what information is likely to communicate with the information on which the system works.

The temptation to use whatever tools we have to hand is particularly dangerous in politics, where the salient tool is legislation backed by enforced compliance. For example, a popular response to a situation where market prices of food are too high is to fix prices. Markets do not respond effectively to such signals, but only to supply and demand. In the case of high prices only some measure to increase supply will solve the problem. The effect of fixing prices is to create a black market in which prices are still higher, because they factor in the costs of defying the law. That is not to say that forcible intervention may never be justified. It may in some circumstances be necessary to confiscate supplies that are being withheld from the market, provided that does not reduce the supply in the long run. However, not every problem has a solution, and it is often hard for us to reconcile ourselves to that fact. The temptation to do something, if only to express our frustration, is very strong. One of the advantages of breaking down questions of policy into specific problems is that when it comes to collective action we may be less inclined to insist on doing something, no matter how inappropriate, when we recognise that we face intractable problems.

Unfortunately, yes-no voting, because it is so information-poor and so often used to force a choice between contrived alternatives, lends itself to inappropriate and counter-productive choices. Democrats accept that consequence because voting is a simple technique that anybody can under-stand and can be applied to almost any subject matter. Democ-racy is seen as 'power to the people', as if the solutions of all our problems were just a matter of who exercises power. How often have we heard it claimed that solving a certain problem is 'just a matter of the political will' to do this or that? What in fact is usually required in those matters is a better understanding of the situation and a general acceptance of appropriate ways of bringing that understanding to bear on the practical question of what precisely is likely to improve it. It is simply impossible for all of us to cultivate a personal understanding of all the problems that arise in a very complex society. We must rely on others whom we can trust in many matters, not because we trust them personally, but because in certain roles they have adequate incentives to do what is required by that role. This central consideration involves a very profound change in our political culture, but not one that can be brought about by preaching some gospel, not even the gospel of demarchy. It will follow on changes in practice, in what come to be accepted as standard practices, not because they give expression to some exciting vision, but because those practices deliver what they purport to deliver in matters that are important to us. Of course, I do need some people to accept the gospel so as to be inspired to set up the necessary experiments.

Effective representation

A key idea in most democratic theory is that the personnel in charge of the institutions of government must be representative of the governed. I concede that about the choice of persons, but not about policies for reasons I have given. To some extent that distinction is acknowledged in present practice. Faced with complex policy decisions, governments often appoint committees to investigate the matter fully, invite submissions from interested groups and arrive at recommendations strictly on the merits of the arguments put to them. Upper houses often justify their distinctive role by appointing bi-partisan committees on certain policy matters. Unfortunately in the context of adversarial politics, such moves are often reduced to tactics. Cynical advice to politicians says: never appoint a committee unless you know what it is going to recommend. If such bodies are to be fully credible, their terms of reference and composition must be decided independently and their coverage of significant areas of policy must become more comprehensive.

However, even if it is agreed that such a regime might produce better policies, that would not respond fully to the profoundly felt need for people to feel that policy decisions are their decisions, not just the deliverances of some impersonal process. I respect that need, and try to argue that it can be met. Admittedly, in my proposals the people to whom the formulation of various policy decisions are entrusted are not a representative sample of the community. They are chosen because they are likely to contribute to sound deliberation. The basic assumption I am making is that the most important way in which people have input into decision-making is by participating in public discussion in which all the diverse considerations that are relevant to the question to be answered (as well, of course, as many irrelevant ones) are brought into play and thoroughly debated. That is the best assurance anybody can have that their concerns have been accorded due significance in the decision process. The status of what the committee concludes depends not on the formula by which its members are chosen, but on its claim to have considered the substance of the various claims to consideration. In any fair process that is all that they can hope for, granted that there has to be some compromise between conflicting considerations.

However, one salutary change to the attitudes of many people that may emerge from thorough discussion is that people may come to realise that their view of their own interests was unduly narrow. The point of full public discussion is not just to enlighten those charged with drawing it to a conclusion. It ought also to educate the other participants and the public more generally. If we value an open society we must recognise that opening up our range of opportunities depends not only on resolving conflicts between people's existing preferences, but in exploring new possibilities that open up when we are prepared to reconsider our preferences. A regime that gives us an active role in that process must balance the protection of our existing interests against the development of new interests.

That point is well illustrated by debates about the questions raised by feminists. There has been a tension throughout those debates between those who insisted on portraying the interests of women in terms of their roles in existing social practices and those who insisted that such roles were precisely what had to change. In the eventual outcome, the social roles did change to a certain extent mainly through social changes and changes in public expectations that only belatedly were reflected in legislation. The whole discussion shows the importance of open-ended discussion. Much discussion drew on the pursuit of equality with men. It gradually became apparent how unsatisfactory that objective was. What was needed was a redefinition of many social roles, not just opening up certain typically male roles to women. While the formal barriers to women's participation in traditionally male roles have largely been eliminated and some redefinition of parenting and household work has begun, there is a great deal that still needs to be done. Similar issues arise in many other contexts, particularly the treatment of minorities. Public debate and a legislative process that is sensitive to that debate rather than to numbers of votes is essential to this opening of the way to creative solutions to problems.

What applies to the self-understanding of social groups also applies to individuals and the ways in which they can benefit from public discussion. Many considerations that they had not previously seen as affecting them are seen as more relevant once the situation is better understood. They are also likely to understand that in many matters they have conflicting interests arising from different roles, and that their ability to solve their personal problems often depends on how the society resolves those differences. The existence of a vigorous public discussion of a problem one share with others enables one to appeal to that discussion in personal relationships. One is not asking for special consideration or favours, but appealing to considerations that are widely accepted as valid.

Such situations are ubiquitous. A woman who has the roles of mother to young children and a demanding professional career inevitably finds those demands imposing problems of reconciling them in many circumstances.

Obviously what she can do in her own particular circumstances depends on the ways in which social decisions structure those roles and the services available to assist people in them. What she can realistically hope for is not that her particular situation should be represented in the decision process but that the process be sensitive to the various considerations that go to constitute it, most of which will have many connections with other situations and problems. What she must hope for is that the policy decisions that emerge allow her room to do what she wants to do and support her in attempting to adapt to the requirements of others. There is a world of difference between a situation when public discussion of such complexities so often reduces to point scoring against one's adversaries and a situation that is directed to finding a resolution to a complex shared problem.

Another aspect of representation is that it inevitably has a particular structure that determines in what respects people are represented. In most democracies representatives are chosen to represent a constituency that is defined by the geographical location of the elector's home. That means that a substantial group of voters who are concentrated in a few key electorates may have a decisive influence on which party wins those seats, while a few such electorates may have a decisive influence on which party wins government. On the other hand a similar number of voters scattered through many electorates may have no influence at all. That leads to gerrymandering in which boundaries between electorates are manipulated by ruling parties to minimise the influence of voters who support their opponents. In policy matters this can be disastrous in favouring certain interests unduly and excluding significant interests from consideration.

A set of permanent institutions designed to give adequate representation to every significant interest in every area of decision so as to ensure that the information flowing through those institutions represented the needs of each and all would be extremely complex and cumbersome. The day may come when computation can manage such a task, but it is beyond our present capacity for registering and interrelating the relevant information. The best we can hope for at the moment is that open public discussion will ensure that when a matter is singled out for decision any substantial interest will find advocates who articulate its needs. Such discussion should normally result in at least a sound picture of the problem of reconciling those interests insofar as they conflict in various ways, and perhaps make some progress towards suggesting solutions to the problem. The many people who are not in a position to articulate their own considerations, including the unborn, in any case have to rely on others spontaneously advocating on their behalf.

Public discussion is likely to be inconclusive because in such discussion the differences between diverse considerations may well emerge clearly, but no particular resolution of those differences may emerge as uniquely preferable. So political parties pick the bits of public discussion that suit their strategies and reject the rest as irrelevant or mistaken. Hence my emphasis on bodies that can claim to develop out of public discussion decisions that can make a plausible claim to be the best way of reconciling the various considerations adduced in the discussion. What precise forms those councils should take is a matter that can be decided only by experience, and it is unlikely that one formula is going to fit all problems. Some are inclined to emphasise the value of having representation of all the interests involved. That gives the body a strong claim to be representative. It also tends to lead to a large body, usually more than a hundred people and to procedures that are formalised to give each person who has something to say the opportunity to do so. In my view such bodies are readily accepted, but their decisions are likely to be unadventurous compromises that may fail to grasp the opportunity to deal with the root causes of the problem. That may well be a sound way of dealing with some problems, especially those that simply do not admit of a decisive solution, but only of shifting adjustments to conflicting considerations.

The sort of body I would like to promote is much smaller, in the interests of much more fluid discussion in which questions can be addressed in depth. Such a body would consist of a dozen people,[1] chosen as a representative sample of the legitimate interests most strongly affected by the problem to be solved, but not of every group that has an interest in it.

---

[1] I must emphasise that this view is based on 'conventional wisdom' about the limits of size of deliberative bodies. What matters is what works in practice in particular contexts. New Democracy Foundation regularly uses juries of about forty members, with considerable success.

Concentrating on the core of the problem, I would hope that they would be inclined to look for ways of getting to solutions that might not be apparent if the emphasis was on compromise. If that were the focus they would be much more likely to consider theoretical analyses that might reveal important aspects of it that are not apparent to observation using established models and categories. Theory, of course, is dangerous. The ambition of the theorist is to show that a very small set of tightly interconnected factors can explain everything about certain phenomena. Applied in practical contexts theories are very likely to lead to the neglect or exclusion of factors about which the theory is silent. I would expect that a group of people strongly affected by the forces at work in their situation would not be inclined to make the mistake of neglecting any of them.

An aspect of representation that has always been important is that it contributes to assuring people that not only their instrumental interests but their expressive interests are given due weight. Experts might arrive at sound decisions where only material, quantifiable interests are involved. Indeed in some such matters they are quite likely to do better than those who are personally involved. But such decisions are socially unacceptable in most contexts. We are concerned not only to provide everybody with a certain amount of living space or access to this or that facility, but also to construct social decisions that express our shared values. We can take pride in an iconic building that is located in our city even though some trans-national corporation built it, without any input from us. People long took pride in their monarch who took little notice of them. But one of the great claims of representative democracy is to give people not just what they need from government, but what they want, to express a common identity. One of the reasons for dissatisfaction with contemporary governments is that they fail to do this. Instead of giving expression to people' views they are seen as manipulating them.

I believe that the remedy for this situation is that policies must be seen to be the outcome of a public debate in which status and power have no place, and various considerations are advanced simply on their merits in as inclusive a perspective as possible. If that debate is to arrive at a conclusion there has to be an adjudication. Counting heads in a referendum is not a good way of deciding on the relative merits of the considerations that have been advanced in the debate. That is best done by people who are prepared to go through the complex and difficult process of arriving at a conclusion that gives as much as possible to each of the points that they see as relevant and important. Because these people are the sort of people who have to bear the various consequences of their decisions, they are not likely to neglect any substantial interest in exploring those consequences. So people should see their decisions as likely to be fair and practical. If the ethos is to take pride in a well governed society people should see those decisions as expressing their aspirations, something with which they profoundly identify in countless different ways.

Admittedly, such an ethos requires a lot of sophistication and tolerance, the opposite of so much traditional politics that feeds on taking sides in conflicts and finding supreme satisfaction in defeating one's enemies. That orientation may be built into our genes by natural selection throughout a long history of settling differences by violent combat. But perhaps we can indulge that predisposition to conflict in imagination as we read the tales of fictional heroes or watch *Star Wars*. Or it can find a ritualised outlet for it on the football field. Living together in constructive enterprises of many and varied kinds in conditions of scarcity is a wonderful achievement. We must appreciate and celebrate the magnificence of it as a collective achievement. Of course, we are the more likely to appreciate it the more experiences we share of how difficult it is. Many, but by no means all of us, must have had that experience, making it a part of our shared understanding of our world. Traditional political cultures sought concerted action on the basis of a unanimity that rested on outlawing most kinds of differences. A rich and inclusive culture must rest on a different sort of agreement, an understanding of how diversity can enrich us all, if only we find ways of handling the problems it poses.

One of the reasons why I believe that it is most important to divorce policy discussion and decision-making from defined jurisdictions, especially geographical ones, is that interests are fluid and that what interests and what considerations are relevant to a specific problem are relative to that problem, not to any fixed grouping of people. If sufficient people are dissatisfied with the way in which a particular problem is identified and discussed, they must be able to set up their own inquiry into it, without any question of their lacking jurisdiction. One might hope that eventually the competing enquiries might agree to cooperate, because their decisions will be more likely to be accepted if they can reach agreement. The possibility of a rival body being set up should be a powerful incentive to one that already exists to make every effort to accommodate the concerns that might lead to a competitor becoming established in a way that leads to a sterile fight for supremacy.

The rhetoric of rationality and morality are bedevilled by the sharp alternatives, truth–falsity and good–evil. We are all inclined to see complex problems as much simpler than they really are, because we look at them from limited perspectives using crude means of identifying what is relevant to dealing with our situation. So we underestimate the difficulties of arriving at a satisfactory solution and particularly of grasping the variety of considerations that affect it. This limitation applies to experts as well as to ordinary people. Economists see problems as reducible to cost-benefit considerations, managers see them as organisational problems, while technicians look for innovative technology for solutions. In the case of services there are normally many different requirements to be met. The task of reconciling these diverse considerations is not easy. If we expect our representatives to do that well, they must be capable and well motivated. That in turn demands that the task we set them be clearly defined and limited.

It is often assumed that ordinary people with no particular expertise are incapable of handling even such problems as the health policy issue I've just mentioned. Probably most people feel that they could not master or interrelate all the considerations involved once they come to see the range of factors that are relevant to decisions on the issues. They become bewildered by the concerns of others about a problem in a genuine effort to reach a practical resolution in the circumstances. Not everybody is capable of such work or motivated to do it well. My firm view is that those we ask to take it on must be volunteers, if not self-nominated, at least encouraged to turn it down if they want to. That means that the sort of people who would serve on deliberative councils are not likely to be typical of most of us. Mostly we find committee work unattractive, for a host of different reasons. The members of a particular council can be all substantially affected by the problem they are called on to address, but it is unlikely that they will be a cross-section of the range of people who are affected by it. There is clearly a danger that the poor, the poorly educated, the diffident, the very old and very young, not being represented, will not be accorded due consideration.

From this point of view such councils cannot be fully democratic. Some dimensions of representation are sacrificed in order to privilege the quest for good decisions. In practice a full and open public discussion should prevent this bias from being dangerous to the unrepresented interests. Many people see it as an obligation to draw attention to the needs of those who cannot speak for themselves. Conscious of their luck in life's lottery they feel a need to help those who lost out. As for the ideal of adequate representation, I believe it rests on a simplistic view of the concept. What is most important is that the interests of people in regard to a matter be adequately represented in proportion to the seriousness of those interests. People deserve to be considered as needing representation in proportion to the danger of a wrong decision affecting them very substantially. A simple blind choice by lot cannot reflect those differences. It may be possible in some contexts to score people on the strength of their various claims to representation in that context, and it may be worth doing so, where that is possible. But the advantages of doing so have to be weighed against the costs in particular contexts. No representative scheme can turn those who cannot articulate their interests into adequate advocates on their own behalf. To repeat my contention, the merits of a council's decision must rest on the arguments in favour of it.

Beyond democracy?

In many matters we need to recognise that our options are shaped by what others do quite independently of their coercing us in any way. We cannot control the externalities arising from many things they do quite legitimately, as when a company closes an unproductive factory, devastating the community built up around it. In such cases it is easy to blame capitalism, but in any changing economy such decisions are inevitable and making fully adequate compensation to those affected is often impossible. A great deal depends on the ambient culture and the expectations it generates. If such events are expected so that workers are used to relocating in pursuit of employment and those who service the needs of the community accept such changes in much the same spirit as changes in the weather, they may accept that they have no title to compensation. In other circumstances, where there are no jobs accessible to the workers the question what to do is not so easily answered, but answers can be developed within the scope of national or regional politics. In a world where all national economies and the lifestyles they support are dependent on a world economy and the productive technologies that it employs, it is impossible to address many problems at national level or by the procedures that we customarily see as democratic.

The problem of how to deal with the effects of our technologies on our ecosystems takes a particularly acute form in the case of genetic engineering. At the moment the regulation of genetic engineering is entirely under the control of national governments, subject to the provisions of agreements about patents and other provisions of international agreements about freedom of trade. On the one hand, firms operating for profit have invested a great deal in research that has resulted in genetically modified crops with many desirable characteristics, ranging from increased yields per acre to resistance to disease and pests. They and their supporters are convinced that it is in the interest of all concerned that those crops be available worldwide and that they be suitably rewarded for their developing them. On the other hand, many people are worried that the consequences of introducing artificially constructed genes into the ecosystem are uncertain and possibly uncontrollable. So many jurisdictions have prohibited planting genetically engineered (GE) crops. In the eyes of supporters of GE this is irrational.

In the modern world it is in practice impossible to prevent the spread of organisms once they are introduced into uncontrolled environments. They are free to interact in every possible way with other organisms. Both the original seeds and new strains that develop from them by natural genetic variations can travel across geographical boundaries on the feathers of birds, the clothing of travellers and adhering to other items of trade. Supporters of GE point out that most of the seeds in question have been so engineered that they are sterile to ensure that farmers have to buy new seeds each year from their supplier if they want to continue with that crop—this means that there is very little likelihood of any of their hybrids or variants surviving and reproducing. But that hardly answers fears about what a diet of genetically sterile food might have on us and other animals. The debate is very inconclusive. Many fears are extremely speculative. There is no particular reason to think those outcomes are likely to happen. On the other hand it is very unclear how we can positively rule them out. In genetics most improbable changes often occur. Most of them are not repeated, much less reproduced on a large scale, but . . .

The issues surrounding GE are bound up with the wider issue of patents. Many free trade agreements involve strict provisions for respecting patents, and negotiations about free trade have often foundered on this issue. It is in the interest of patent holders to construe the scope of a patent as broadly as possible. So they try to patent not just the substance or technique that they have shown to be effective but many similar substances or techniques that seem likely to admit of similar applications. Again, they often seek to perpetuate a patent beyond its expiry date by introducing improved versions of their product as deserving new patent protection. Patents belong to the undesirable category of monopoly rents, which require strong justification. Obviously, there is a lot of room for disagreement about what constitutes sufficient justification in very many cases.

Some of the issues about patents were highlighted a few years ago when a US company was granted a patent on a gene. From one point of view that was nothing unusual. Companies have frequently been granted patents on the use of some naturally occurring substance for certain purposes, normally on the understanding that restrictions on its use do not interfere with established uses of it for other purposes. But surely not the basic keys to life itself! The patent was eventually invalidated, leaving a great deal of dissatisfaction about how the patent system had developed.

In pharmaceuticals the validity of patents granted in one country has frequently been challenged when attempts are made to enforce them in other countries. A very large proportion of pharmaceutical patents are held in the US, where most consumers are accustomed to paying high prices to compensate the patent owners. Many of those medications are urgently required in countries where hardly anybody can afford those prices. The manufacturing cost of supplying these items are often quite small, and some poorer countries have flourishing pharmaceutical industries that can market them cheaply. Such producers often allege that the patent holders spend less on research than on promoting their products and protecting their monopolies. The patent holders retort that much of the expense of marketing a drug lies in exhaustive tests to ensure its safety, optimal dosage and compliance with tight regulations in their home market that do not exist in many other jurisdictions.

There is little prospect of these issues being settled satisfactorily as long as the granting and enforcement of patents is left to national authorities or to bilateral treaties between countries with diametrically opposed interests in every aspect of the matter. Even though the long-term interests of both various producers and consumers may tend to converge, in negotiating treaties the negotiators are constrained by the short-term politics of the nations involved. The politicians cannot afford to be seen as sacrificing the salient interests of their citizens to some hypothetical future. In both business and electoral politics short-term considerations inevitably tend to prevail. The future is always uncertain, while the present is undeniable. A satisfactory world system in this domain would enable a country with a flourishing pharmaceuticals industry like India to gain access to world markets, could encourage the US research industry to devote more attention to products that have little domestic market but are urgently needed over much of the world, and so on. Clearly, what is needed is an authority that over time can develop the host of incremental changes to present practices that will favour the long term interests of all concerned.

My suggestion is that the personnel of such a body should be chosen by lot from a large panel of suitably qualified people nominated by interested parties, including consumers, prescribers, and producers. There would need to be a formula ensuring a reasonable spread of members among those various interests. Continuity and renewal would be assured by changing members one by one on fixed terms. The authority of the body would be grounded simply in its capacity to deliver acceptable solutions to the particular range of issues it confronts. In order to succeed in achieving that recognition the members would need to see themselves as charged not to prevail over their opponents but as negotiating to achieve as fair and practical a set of decisions as they could.

Such an institution is not democratic, if by democratic one means deciding issues by the majority vote of those individuals who choose to vote. There is no choice of competing alternatives. The only question is whether or not to accept the conclusion of the committee. As I envisage the process of decision, the elected government would have the final responsibility for that choice, just as it has today. If the conclusion of the deliberative process was widely accepted, voting could only be the sort of plebiscitary endorsement that dictators have sought. If there is any doubt about public support, the choice is inevitably going to be framed as a choice between what favours one party as opposed to the others. It invites the sort of spoiler voting that rejects a sound compromise simply because, for example, it involves an immediate rise in the price of certain items while the benefits lie in the future. Even sophisticated voters, baffled by the complexities of such issues as what constitutes a fair return to the pharmaceutical companies, are likely to fall back on voting for what appears to promise cheaper drugs next year. The likelihood of getting sound decisions from referenda on such matters is minimal.

In many traditions that consequence is willingly accepted. They acknowledge that there will be cases where constructive collective action is impeded by voting that is imprudently negative and shortsighted. They insist that the greater danger is that of tyranny or at least of the use of inefficient and unnecessary compulsion to deal with problems that could be handled in better ways. Government means compulsion and liberty is a matter of minimising compulsion. We must make it possible for people to reject compulsion, except where it is absolutely necessary. This view does focus on a real danger, but, as I shall argue, it rests on a false conception of authority as compulsion and of collective decisions as struggles for power. I agree that they often come down to that. The question is, does it have to be that way? In essence my claim is that a certain amount of compulsion is needed in the administration and enforcement of policy decisions, but is neither necessary nor helpful in arriving at them. However, in discussing policy questions one very important consideration to be weighed against others is the amount of coercion involved in implementing them.

The problem of public goods

Economists define public goods as those that are affected by market failure. In particular they insist on two characteristics of such goods, that they are 'non-rival' and 'non-excludable'. That is to say, my enjoying the good in question does not necessarily diminish your enjoying it and I can't exclude you from enjoying it. The most important public goods come free, like the air we breathe, or are by-products of what people do for their personal reasons. A market is a by-product of a lot of individual transactions that are not intended to construct a market. Cultural goods like a literary tradition are a product of many people doing their own thing. It is impossible to put a price on most of them, because nobody has to pay for using them.

However, many public goods can be supplied only by organised action using inputs that do need to be purchased on the market. What they cost may be clear, but what they are worth is not. Public services, roads and armies are obvious examples. Collectively we have to pay for them by taxation, whether we use them or not. We justify our all being obliged to contribute to the public purse by the fact that we are all dependent on living in a well-provided and well-regulated society, and all of the goods financed out of the public purse contribute in a variety of ways to the public good as a whole. Still, even if we accept that point, we would love to know whether spending from the public purse on some specific project is getting good value for the money it costs.

Economists usually think that expenditure on public projects tends to be too much or too little. So they have developed ingenious ways of making cost–benefit assessments of particular projects. These depend on putting prices on the benefits as well as on the costs. It is assumed that pricing the benefits is achieved by summing the benefits to each individual user. Suppose it is a question of extending a railway to new potential customers. You estimate the number of people who are likely to be attracted to the area when the trains become available and the average price they will be prepared to pay for using them, as if you were an investor putting up the required capital. Is the investment likely to make a profit? Simple arithmetic?

As a matter of public policy it is not so simple, as I have already shown. There are many externalities, consequences that affect other goods favourably or unfavourably, that neither a user nor an entrepreneur has to pay for directly. A big increase in the population of the area means financing the extension of many other public services such as schools, sewers and hospitals throughout the area. So extending the area served by public transport may be a much more costly way of accommodating a larger population than encouraging higher density accommodation in areas already served by such facilities. Pricing such factors becomes increasingly complicated, not least because it involves changing preferences as well as many unpredictable costs and benefits. The large factory that was going to employ people in the new suburb is not built. People who used to think they must live in a detached cottage discover the advantages of condominiums. People change their ideas about where is a good place to live.

That is not to say that cost-benefit analyses are useless. Even if we attach great importance to the expressive value of some public good, we need to be clear about what it costs. Cost analyses enable one to construct sophisticated computer models with which one can trace the consequences of varying each factor in relation to variations in other factors. So we are not limited to deciding on what assumptions to adopt and assessing projects on that basis. This is an enormous advance, particularly in attempting to evaluate the effects of many uncertainties on different proposals. It may show clearly that a certain attractive proposal only remains attractive if the major costs and benefits of particular factors all stay within a certain range of variations over a long period. Gambling on that happening may be clearly too risky. So that proposal must be ruled out. Even when there are important factors that cannot be priced at all, it is normally very useful to have those that can be dealt with in relation to an economic model of those factors that can be clearly analysed.

There is no general metric in terms of which the costs and benefits of public goods can be compared. What we value about them is culturally relative and context-dependent. The only way to arrive at agreement about their worth is by discussion and negotiation. Ultimately that is true of money also. It is only the stability of market prices that gives a sort of objectivity to monetary prices.

The market works so well because it deals in what can be produced, stored, and exchanged freely. Where things that cannot be produced are concerned, such as paintings by past masters, prices are just a matter of fashion. To some extent that is true of money itself. In contemporary culture what matters most to many people is not money but time, especially free time. For the producers, entrepreneurs and workers, time is money. Labour-time is bought and sold. But for most consumers the point is reversed: money is time. It enables us to buy time we can use as we like, mainly in activities that have no market value, but mean a great deal to us personally. The nearest we have to a metric of the value a person places on any activity is the amount of time that they wish to devote to it.

In bourgeois culture the major expression of success in life is conspicuous consumption of the best that money could buy in housing, clothing and services. In post-bourgeois culture it is the freedom to engage in whatever one finds satisfying or entertaining. In these days of television and smart phones entertainment is relatively cheap. There is much less point in accumulating money at the expense of time. But mere entertainment soon becomes boring. People look for more active ways of using their time, especially in activities that are seen as enhancing meaning. Such agreed meanings are social creations. They grow out of basic drives, but they get a particular shape, embodied in particular patterns of action and symbolism, only by convention. In many instances these conventions arise out of the ways in which certain connections become established in the course of people's uncoordinated activities. Their meanings are entirely internal to that web of connections, as in all the games and roles we play. These conventions constitute the components of cultures. They are historically specific and to some extent arbitrary, but rich in shared meanings and possibilities of shared satisfactions. Shared satisfactions are reassuring because they are validated by agreement about their value.

When we find a need to construct particular public goods or regulate pre-existing ones, there is no scientific way of making the basic choices involved.

The factors are nearly all unquantifiable. How happy we are with a particular suggestion is often a matter of feelings we find hard to articulate. If we are happy with most aspects of the context into which a new element is to be introduced, we will be reluctant to risk altering it. On the other hand, if we are dissatisfied with the present situation we are much more likely to experiment boldly. There is no clear answer in such cases, but often we must reach agreement by conversation and negotiation or else have it imposed on us without regard to our feelings. Demarchy is premised on the belief that it is possible for us to do this in a salutary and satisfying way, provided we concentrate on specifics rather than grand schemes of social organisation.

A great deal of ingenuity has gone into devising ways of supplying traditionally private goods in the form of public goods (by socialists) and traditionally public goods in the form of private goods (by libertarians). The early socialists aspired to supply as many goods as possible as one big happy family, guided by the maxim 'from each according to their capacities, to each according to their needs'. Even on the scale of very small closed communities that proved very difficult. It worked in complex groups only where some powerful authority made the requisite allocations of tasks and benefits. The present trajectory is in the opposite direction, towards privatisation in the interest of efficiency and freedom of choice. Unfortunately, in strictly economic terms efficiency comes down to profitability, which is not a satisfactory measure of many of the aspects that we most value in things. At best it reflects our preferences between the limited alternatives that it suits the producers to offer us. Organisations that supply public goods through market transactions, such as banks and insurance companies, often become too important to be punished by allowing their losses to destroy them. So the profits from supplying public goods are often distributed in accordance with the maxim 'privatise the gains, socialise the losses'. Big corporations like banks and public utilities are too important to be let fail. So they are bailed out from the consequences of their own poor decisions, while continuing to flourish on a more or less guaranteed income from services that are socially indispensible.

The social problem concerning for-profit capital investment in supplying public goods is to ensure adequate investment where it is needed without creating incentives to distort those needs in order to increase profits. In regard to many public utilities that are very capital intensive, the incentive needs to be a guarantee that the return on capital will be satisfactory, but no greater than with other secure investments. The standard way of giving such a guarantee is to set maximum prices that these enterprises are permitted to charge and allow the entrepreneur to pocket the difference between the cost of production and the price charged for it. The maximum is set as a standard mark-up on the usual cost of production. That is essentially a cost-plus contract, where the costs are set by the producer. In the longer term it is usually more profitable for the producer to increase capital investment unnecessarily, if that investment will continue to be rewarded in spite of its inefficiency, than to reduce costs and run the risk that the maximum price allowed will be reduced to eliminate excess profits. As an acquaintance of mine, an industrialist who had made huge profits from cost-plus contracts during WW2, used to say: 'I wouldn't give a cost-plus contract to the Angel Gabriel himself!'

Apart from ideology, the main force driving towards the privatisation of the production of public goods is that states need the money from selling those operations to meet other commitments, while there is ample private capital looking for profitable investments. It is interesting that after WW2 the rush to nationalise key industries in Europe was justified to those who didn't agree with socialist ideology by pointing out that sufficient private capital was not available. Now the position is reversed. The huge growth of returns to capital since the eighties is something that has not been adequately explained. In his day Marx thought he could explain the accumulation of capital in terms of the dominant economic theory of value at that time. The labour theory of value is now obsolete, and Marx's theory does not fit the operating mechanisms in contemporary economies. There seems to be no agreed explanation of the present situation. What most commentators have emphasised are the political rather than strictly economic factors that favour the disproportionate rewards to capital. So most proposed remedies look to introducing controls of one kind or another over financial institutions. I'll return to this later.

One of the most important problems about investment in major public capital goods is that of encouraging the development of an infrastructure that is both economically efficient and socially and ecologically sound. In the short run the cheapest way of supplying our energy needs is to use existing technologies that rely on fossil fuels. Not only does that have environmental costs that threaten to be unsustainable, but in the longer term the newer technologies turn out to be cheaper, both because as the technology develops they become cheaper in terms of capital cost and because their running costs are small and the fuel is free. How long a perspective we adopt is a difficult question. Both capital markets and governments that face re-election are driven to concentrate on short-term perspectives. That short-term focus is most inappropriate in regard to most public goods. Any adequate way of handling the problems of investment in public goods has to face the question of how to decide what we want in our particular public goods, and how we are to reconcile our diverse preferences. Economic considerations are not enough.

I have been emphasising the positive aspect of public goods, but a lot of the goods supplied by organised activity, particularly by bureaucratic institutions, are directed to averting public evils: crime, natural disasters, epidemics, conflagrations and other dangers that are beyond the control of most people. Their value consists in the absence of an evil, which is hardly perceptible if all goes well, but their costs are obvious. They often place restrictions on what we can do and impose some degree of surveillance on everybody that is irksome. The benefits are intangible, the costs apparent. These services are supplied by bureaucracies, which are always open to accusations of inflating their own importance and providing sinecures for their personnel. Measuring their efficiency is extremely difficult to monitor, and in the case of policing there is also the inevitable danger of the abuse of power.

In these and many other matters, good policy decisions are not enough. A watch needs to be kept on the continuing dangers of overspending, corruption and abuse of power to which bureaucracies of most kinds are congenitally prone. Full transparency and public attention is needed, and there is a persistent interest in insisting on it in the media. There is also, I believe, in many contexts a place for councils similar to demarchic policy bodies to exercise a continuing supervision of some bureaucracies and to comment on their performance in a more comprehensive and balanced way than the media can provide. To some extent there already exist institutionalised bodies that perform surveillance functions, but they often develop an excessively legalistic approach to their task or become too closely identified with the institutions they supervise. Careers in the watchdogs become linked with careers in the institutions they watch.

Against a certain moralism

By moralism I mean two linked tendencies: ascribing faults that are the result of poorly designed procedures to the failure of individuals to do what they ought to do, and designing procedures by applying moral consideration to oversimplified models of what is reasonable to expect of those who operate them. One moralistic view I want to examine is that all citizens have both an equal right and an equal duty to vote on the question of who is to be entrusted with sovereign authority. What that doctrine and others like it do is to construct moral prescriptions on the basis of an impracticable model of social life. When those prescriptions fail, the blame falls on those who do not conform to them instead of on the model that underlies the prescriptions. We are distracted from seeking better solutions to the problem. Even in the most enthusiastically democratic countries, very many conscientious citizens don't bother to vote or give serious consideration to the issues. They observe correctly that one vote in a mass vote is insignificant or that none of the alternatives deserves their endorsement. Or they don't pretend to understand most of the issues. So they think of what the political system imposes on them as something like the weather. There's nothing you can do about it. Just roll with the punches or perhaps kick up a fuss when it really hurts, in the hope the politicians will do something to keep you quiet.

In Australia and some other countries we fine people for not voting, or at least going through the requisite motions. That emphasises the view that being eligible to vote entails a responsibility to contribute to the process of making good decisions. It does seem to have some salutary effects. The poor are usually more likely to find voting futile than those who do well under the existing system. So, in many jurisdictions, they tend to stay away in droves, with the result that political parties are under no pressure to address their preferences. The poor get what their betters think they ought to get. In a generally affluent society many assume that if people who are capable of working are poor, it is usually their fault. To encourage them to vote is to encourage irresponsibility. The majority, who are not poor, are against indulging them. No party that wants to appeal to the majority can afford to offer much to the poor if they don't vote.

For similar reasons to those that favour compulsory voting, most advocates[2] of choosing representatives by lot insist that it is necessary that every citizen be required to serve if chosen in order to give a balanced representation. It is obviously a huge imposition on many people to demand that they devote an important slice of their lives to the job that politicians are expected do full-time. Most, I think, would soon realise that they are being asked to make decisions on matters that are too difficult for them to handle. Many people who are very conscious of their debts to the community will rightly think that there are better ways for them to repay those debts than attempting to address the whole range of questions of public policy.

It is dangerous to assume that the defects in our politics are due to the voters or the politicians failing to do their duty. Every regime in history has fended off criticism of the system by claiming that it would work perfectly well if only the people who run it were more conscientious. Of course, many failures of governments to deliver the goods are due to the delinquencies of those who exercise power, the corrupt, the lazy, the frivolous and the fanatics. But any regime is a framework of incentives to perform certain roles in the system. The roles must be such that it is possible for the players to perform well in them and the incentives must not be perversely counterproductive or inadequate. If positive incentives are not effective in encouraging players to want to perform well, punishing failure is not likely to be effective either. In any social role the basic incentive to perform well must be that the performer wants to be recognised as performing well and to deserve that recognition.

Where many regimes have failed is that they have forbidden the sort of critical assessment of the performance of officials that is needed to give substance to assessments of their

---

[2]   Notably those who call themselves *Kleroterians*. See the forum Equality by lot at Wordpress.com.

worth. They honoured certain people simply for their occupy-
ing a certain role and treated criticism of their performance as
undermining the importance of that role. The performer was
supposed to act well out of a sense of duty or to be answerable
to some higher power and to nobody else. Popular judgment
was irrelevant, based on ignorance and sinfulness. Such
incentives were often perverse, encouraging the players to have
an absurd belief in their own capacities and to construe their
role in completely arbitrary ways. In the twentieth century,
authoritarian regimes were grounded on such constructs as the
leader who was the incarnation of the true destiny of the
people. The existing population was inevitably disqualified
from criticising the leader. They could not shake off their
subservience to their petty interests or the bad habits of the
past. The leader alone could be trusted without reservation.

The powerful seduction to which so many succumbed at
that time is often legitimated by a false moralism, in this case
the assumption that moral excellence is a matter of devotion to
some end that transcends ordinary human objectives. Liberal
democracy is seen as at best a grubby struggle between
materialistic interests to achieve their own petty selfish ends. It
serves a capitalist society in which money is god and the
market the invisible hand of god's providence. Its vaunted
freedom is simply the right to chase money. By making all
higher goals irrelevant it condemns us to be slaves of the
system. A lot of people feel such disgust with the system but do
not fall for the claims of political leaders to remedy it or
supplant it. They seek personal salvation from a mean society
in religion, knowledge, the arts and above all in personal
relationships, especially romantic love. A dichotomy is
established in which politics as a nasty game is contrasted with
personal relationships in which our better selves can express
themselves. Demarchy challenges that assumption. Politics can
be morally fulfilling.

I want to question the view that it is necessary for people to
be devoted to some transcendent end without which politics is
and can only be a selfish, materialistic power game. If the

apparatus of government is dedicated to legislating and administering sound policies that foster the interests of all the components of the social system, the result should be a win-win, not only for most of the particular interests affected by those policies but for the community as a whole. A social order in which the greatest possible variety of activities that people find worthwhile flourishes is a public good that everybody can enjoy and value. Although the aggregate result will not be designed to express some particular moral philosophy or objective, both the particular policies and the overall result can be expected to embody the whole range of moral concerns. The analogy I want to stress is that of a complex ecosystem that can be admired both as a whole and in the various organisms that constitute it. The whole has no single purpose or function. It has to be valued for what it is. Its constituents are to some extent characterised by their contributions to the whole, but have their own intrinsic value. As living things they are all mortal and are driven to grow, realise their potential, adapt to the circumstances in which they are placed and above all to reproduce themselves.

The global whole of human society serves no further purpose we can determine beyond developing its own potential, but its component individuals and sub-groups do develop purposes that relate not just to their individual growth, adaptation and reproduction, but to collective activities and achievements that go beyond their individual capacities. They can cooperate to gather, process, store and communicate ideas that enable them to invent whole systems of new uses for each other and for many elements of the world. Each of those creations has its own point, intrinsic to itself, just like the people who produce them. In this they resemble the components of an ecosystem. Whether an organism in fact grows, adapts or reproduces itself is entirely a matter of physical events over which it has no control. Human beings, on the other hand, while no less dependent on chance events, do have some capacity to manipulate some of those events because they can amass, process and apply knowledge. The course of biological evolution is entirely determined by uncontrolled events. The course of human evolution is to some extent in our own hands and so too is much of the course of biological evolution, because of the development of our knowledge of genetics and so many other factors.

The earth's resources are limited. In the course of the ordinary natural processes, valuable organisms fail to survive. Similarly, not all human activities can survive, but at both the biological and the social level we can increase the survival rates of what we want to survive by eliminating many of the organisms and activities that are inimical to them and developing adaptations to changed circumstances. To do that we have to develop our knowledge of how things work and organise ourselves to apply it effectively. It is crucial to understanding what we can do to grasp the significance of the fact that all reliable knowledge is very specific. Each of the basic laws of physics, even if they apply to our whole universe, is about only one specific factor in it, such as gravity. All scientific medicine is a matter of isolating some specific pattern of interactions that constitutes a disease and finding ways of controlling certain key factors that produce that pattern. Effective action is always a matter of very specifically identified problems and precisely targeted solutions to them. It is necessary to identify the relevant level of description if the correct form of analysis is to be chosen. In some connections ice can be treated just like any other solid of comparable density. In others it has to be treated in terms of its chemical composition. In some connections a person is just a mouth to be fed, in others, a dangerous criminal.

It is clear that nobody can guarantee that treating the problems of living together by attending to specific problems that we can understand and deal with effectively will be successful in solving all our problems. But there is no other way that is less dangerous. The trouble with the categories in terms of which we describe, analyse and attempt to control factors in human affairs is that they correlate at best only roughly with the sort of underlying causal factors that we can identify and deal with. The larger the scope of the phenomenon that we deal with, the more the vagueness and lack of precision in the concepts available to us is likely to matter. The broad hypothesis on which my approach to our problems is based is that it is often possible to get at least provisional agreement about what steps to take in dealing with a particular problem in given circumstances, even in the absence of agreement about the generalisations in terms of which different groups of us think about it, because we come to recognise that the particular factors we describe differently are in fact the same, at least for practical purposes, in the context. So what is an insoluble problem when addressed on a large scale may admit of piecemeal solutions in particular contexts. A certain pragmatism may succeed where a more ambitious approach would not.

Authority

Authority is invested in a person or group or a procedure when the fact that it has made a certain decision is a strong reason for people to decide voluntarily to follow that decision. Even when people are agreed in general about a common objective, they will frequently either disagree or be undecided about what particular option would best realise it, or the best path to achieving it. Where coordinated action is needed to avoid collective failure, invoking authority is the normal way of resolving disagreement and indecision. In most matters in everyday social life the authority that is relevant is convention. Ways of acting often acquire authority as the proper or correct way for no better reason than that people agree that obeying them is preferable to trying to change them, perhaps simply because doing so is not worth the effort as far as any individual is concerned. Many, perhaps most, of our conventions are the product of historical accident. Nevertheless, because conventions matter to us in regulating ways of communicating and coordinating action, they are open to rational assessment.

There is rarely an answer to what is the best alternative to an existing practice, but there are very many that are unacceptable. So, if a change is to be made there needs to be an authority that chooses between the acceptable alternatives. In a variety of contexts certain people manage to achieve sufficient salience for their personal choice to be sufficient to induce others to follow them. They set the fashion, and the penalty of ignoring fashion is to send wrong messages to others. But such salience is fragile. Authority is most secure when the body exercising it makes its decisions on the best available evidence, using the best available decision procedures. Such authority is the more necessary as the considerations involved are more important. But it is always in some degree arbitrary. The larger its scope and the more important its decisions and the more strictly they are enforced, the more dangerous that element of arbitrariness is. There is good reason to minimise large and powerful concentrations of authority, especially when they enforce their decisions by severe penalties.

In our present world order states are the supreme authorities, capable of overriding all other authorities and many preferences of individuals. States prohibit people from doing certain things they want to do and order them to do things they don't want to do. Both of these operations are costly and inefficient. That constitutes one of the problems with politics as we know it. A lot of people inevitably get away with failing to conform to those prohibitions and commands. Enormous resources go into futile attempts at enforcement on the one hand and evasion on the other. There are many unforeseen consequences, most of which are undesirable. These consequences play out in a number of ways. People need to see commands as both sensible and effective if they are to conform to them willingly. What seems sensible may not be effective and what is effective may not seem sensible in the light of some of its consequences. Prohibitions and commands need to be interpreted and applied in a variety of circumstances — often unforeseen circumstances. Give a lot of discretion to those charged with applying your directives and you may achieve not a desirable flexibility and responsiveness, but corruption and arbitrariness. Define what your agents have to do too rigidly and the model soon becomes unworkable or at least inappropriate to changed situations, as, for example, when your commands are flouted on a massive scale (the 'war against drugs', Prohibition etc.).

Criminalisation and enforcement by punishment have their place where a strong temptation exists to ignore or flout important injunctions. Even in such cases they are often not the best option. In the absence of any agreement by certain minorities that the regime is fair, adversarial democracy is often unable to come up with anything better. Where systematic reliance on punishment leads to sending millions of citizens to prison for a postgraduate course in crime, the state's efforts are futile, very expensive and counterproductive. Communities in which a criminal subculture flourishes need to be led to see better prospects for themselves, not crushed by jailing a large percentage of their young people. They need to be given confidence that they are respected, and given the opportunity to construct acceptable lives for themselves. That requires a certain degree of multiculturalism in which cultures are not separate unitary entities, but consist of many strands, most of which are shared with others. My proposals, I hope, are capable of giving practical form to such a conception of cultures and communities.

Preoccupation with command and compliance, crime and punishment, results in a very inadequate picture of authority. There are many authorities on which our societies depend that operate without issuing commands, except within the organisation. They are engaged in setting standards, issuing warnings, authenticating knowledge, disseminating information, providing coordination, organising support, arbitrating conflicts, offering assistance and making awards. Many such bodies monopolise the field in which they operate simply because there is no point in challenging them. The International Olympic Committee, the Red Cross and many other such organisations exercise powerful authority without having the power to issue commands or punish non-compliance. The only penalty for non-conformity is being out on one's own. They get their authority not from states, but from the standing that their work enjoys in the light of the purpose it serves.

Many organisations that were originally established by political authorities to administer certain agreements acquire de facto independence from their original masters. This is particularly the case for many international authorities, especially where the issues they decide are of a scientific or technical character. Our way of life depends on bodies that govern the assignment of broadcast wave bands, internet addresses, postal cooperation and a host of other matters. There is sometimes, however, a need for supervision of such authorities that is not being met under present arrangements but could be met by my proposals. I will later discuss an instance that illustrates this point.

Many bodies that have merely advisory status make decisions that come to have as much force as a command. Obvious examples are aviation safety and control of epidemics. The cost of rejecting their advice is too high to ignore. Individuals and organisations that ignore authoritative advice suffer a decline in respect for their own authority. However, governments and other institutions often do ignore authoritative advice about long-term consequences because they are held to account only in the short term and only on very restricted criteria. I argue that what is needed to tackle many problems is a complex of diverse authorities, each dealing with some particular issue that is not being tackled adequately by existing authorities. Such authorities must consider all matters that are relevant to the problem with which they are concerned. It is not a matter of designing some very complex machinery that will guarantee every possible contingency is covered. What is needed is a flexible and responsive way of meeting old and new problems, which is not dominated by short-term power struggles. Such bodies will need to acquire sufficient authority to shame politicians into taking them seriously. They can do this by establishing a recognised claim to sound decision-making.

The authority that a particular body exercises in a particular community on a specific issue is always a matter of convention, often tacit. Conventions change as opinions, problems, hopes and fears change. Even the most sacred texts are open to many interpretations. But not just anything goes. Our conventions must be sensitive to moral, economic and social considerations rather than ideologies and power struggles. For some matters, we need to establish bodies that can give clear, trustworthy expression to expert opinion, where lay opinion is incompetent. For most matters, however, we need to stimulate frank public discussion and find a way of articulating the results of that discussion. Adversarial politics often closes off constructive discussion. The opposing parties frame the issues in terms of caricatures and myths that suit their political strategies rather than the specific problems in question. They seek to manipulate people rather than inform them. Such tactics can succeed in many cases, even when people are aware of being manipulated, because public discussion cannot break free of its adversarial context. Arguments are evaluated on the basis of suspicions about the political motivations of those who advance them. Most people inevitably lack the resources to evaluate the evidence for themselves. There seems to be no source that they can trust. Surveys of people's personal opinions are usually inadequate to correct this narrowness, since most citizens are inevitably not very well informed about the ramifications of proposals. In any case the questions that are put to them are set in the context of the conflicting claims of the parties.

In what follows, I use the term 'libertarian' in a very general sense to refer to all of those who oppose, in the name of liberty, any extension of the range of state authority. That covers both Thatcherite conservatives and near-anarchist free marketeers. They tend to share a very statist conception of authority, which provides strong reasons for seeing it as detrimental to liberty. They differ about how much authority is justified in contemporary conditions. They also share a lot of confidence in the capacity of custom to provide an adequate framework to regulate what people are entitled to expect from each other without the need for regulatory bodies. The conservatives put their trust in tradition, while the radicals rely on rational self-interest. I shall argue that such views are inadequate, but that the alternative is not state power, as they assume.

By contrast, I want to put a great deal of stress on the potential of very specialised authoritative bodies that do not exercise coercion. On the international scale they can be seen not as overriding the authority of nation states, but as facilitating agreements between them. They use persuasion to remedy the deficiencies of our existing political procedures. In a global society where new problems are emerging with frightening rapidity it seems obvious that customs developed by very homogeneous communities in much more restricted contexts are unlikely to be capable of tackling these novel problems. In practice advocates of established customs are reduced to denying the existence, or at least the urgency, of problems they cannot tackle, such as our role in dealing with climate change or the international monetary system. It is true, of course, that such an outcome involves changes in the political cultures of existing states, and that there is no possibility of first converting those states to these changes and then proceeding to put them into practice as a matter of policy. Changes in practice must come first. What I expect is that some particular bodies in some specific matters may succeed in setting standards or measures that most nations find it expedient to adopt. These cases may encourage them to adopt similar procedures in other matters, so they will come to see them as normal and normative in dealing with a certain range of situations. The only way that international law is enforced is by some nations agreeing to enforce it. But its authority is not negligible.

The psychology of choice

As I noted earlier, we usually find freedom of spontaneity more attractive than freedom of choice, which can be onerous. What is very attractive is being able to make choices spontaneously, enjoying the variety of options offered to us, but being free to choose spontaneously, without having to deliberate about the consequences of choosing one option rather than another. We like being able to choose from a menu as the mood takes us, without having to worry about our diet. In many contexts we expect both government and the market to assure us of such freedom. When we go to buy a new car most of us assume that the fact that a model survives in a competitive market shows that it is competitively priced. At the same time we assume that it complies with government safety requirements and emissions standards. So we can safely make our choice simply on what appeals to us. We would like to be able to 'buy' public policies just as easily, so that we might go about our activities without having to worry about such matters as the social consequences of the choices open to us.

There is nothing irrational or reprehensible about this general preference. We could not possibly each assess all the issues in public policy and arrive at compromises with the views of others by personal discussion. We have to trust some decision-process to arrive at acceptable decisions. The simplest option is to entrust all those decisions to a single authority on the model of a nation as like a person and the government as that person's soul or brain integrating the deployment of its various abilities to serve the needs and aspirations of the whole. Unfortunately that leads both to concentrating excessive power, with all its inherent dangers, and to choices that neglect most of the potential of things. In animals like us the various organs that make up our bodies are naturally integrated to promote the survival, growth and reproduction of the whole. But communities of organisms like ecosystems and societies consist of many different organisms whose objectives are their own growth and reproduction, not that of the society or ecosystem. But by developing in novel ways they open up new possibilities to other organisms and to the system as a whole.

That does not mean that the interests of the components are all antagonistic to each other. On the contrary, they are interdependent and adapted to one another in a host of different ways, as well as competing against each other in many other respects. This lack of unity is not something that can be avoided. Nor is it undesirable. Out of the interplay of these processes of adaptation and conflict, new forms of life emerge, creating new possibilities, some destructive, others creative. Human beings have a capacity to organise extraordinarily powerful forms of effective action for both construction and destruction, but we cannot rely on any process to ensure that these powers work for our various interests over the whole range of interactions in play in various contexts. As with our health, the best we can do is identify the particular forces that damage or advantage us and look for ways of dealing with them. Doing that effectively cannot be left to spontaneous reactions. Those reactions are naturally directed at symptoms, not what causes them. Each problem has to be investigated in its own terms, looking for the specific causes of the problem and for acceptable ways of dealing with it. I claim that committees of a certain kind are generally best in the role of deciding what should be done in such matters.

Recent fashion has been to highlight the importance of the manager as innovative leader in contrast to the dead hand of committees. In part that emphasis was justified by the way in which rapid technological change, especially in communications, data processing and transportation, was accelerating the speed with which many decisions had to be made. That put a lot of weight on the capacity of the CEO to make quick decisions and mobilise the organisation to accept and implement them. A sluggish or incompetent CEO could do untold damage. In popular ideology there was a tendency to revive the 'leadership principle', so dear to the great dictators in every age, which attributes everything good about the organisation to the vision of the leader and everything bad to those who fail to follow that direction. Most people like identifying with a leader who can project an exciting sense of superiority in which they can share by displaying their appreciation of the leader's vision. We are all familiar with the very human need for inspired leadership in a great variety of contexts: religious, political, sporting and even business. In an era where the mass media can hardly avoid portraying differences in policy and achievement as differences of personalities, this obfuscation is difficult to resist.

Closely allied with the functional need for leadership is the need to project the status of the organisation via the social status of its leader. The organisation manifests its own self-esteem in providing its leader with the trappings of high social standing. Even the most humble and ascetic bishops have been required to don a certain ostentatious garb and engage in social activities that befit their importance. Nowadays the organisation seeks to express its own importance by paying its CEO a salary commensurate with that of others in similar positions. Regimes of this sort are extremely dangerous. The cult of quick, intuitive, decision is completely inappropriate in deciding policy.

Unfortunately in many business and political contexts, where leaders must face judgement at the next AGM or the next election, they are bound to pursue short-term interests, often at the expense of longer-term and more important considerations. They promote inferior merchandise under prestigious labels, leverage the organisation's assets in risky ventures or plunge the nation into dangerous commitments in order to be seen to 'get things done', which is the mark of the 'true leader'. I shall return to these problems later. Meanwhile, it is clear that the tendency towards disentangling responsibilities and allocating them to councils that I am advocating is designed to minimise the role of grand leadership in society. That is not to deny the importance of appropriate kinds of leadership in specific initiatives in very many contexts. Much less is it to deny the importance of shared visions of the future. What is dangerous is to invest them in a single focus or person.

Sound institutions draw a distinction in practice between policy matters that are best decided by deliberative bodies and operational decisions where individual leadership must prevail, since quick decisions are needed. Clearly in global concerns the representative structures and deliberative capacities of the bodies that handle such matters are crucial and a long-term perspective is essential. Their function is to give practical expression to the verdict of public discussion, not to lead it in some pre-set direction. Leadership has a role in dramatising neglected considerations. That is an important element in discussion, as long as it is kept in perspective. In an open society the most fruitful ideas come not from institution-alised leadership but from creative individuals and small groups inspiring others to follow their example. The final decisions on public policies need to reflect a compromise between diverse interests rather than the sort of single interest that leaders can project.

Transforming committee work

I have spoken of councils rather than committees or juries, because committees have a bad name. It often seems that the only people who like serving on committees are the people that nobody else wants on a committee, the self-important bores, the one-track activists, those who 'vote with the strength' and those who have nothing better to do. To have to sit for hours being polite to such bores, trying in vain to get them to focus on the real issues or listen to what you have to say, is not an attractive proposition. It is not surprising that people tend to have little confidence in committees. They trust prime ministers and individual ministers rather than cabinet, CEOs rather than boards of directors, mayors rather than councils, and so on. They feel that an individual who is personally responsible for her decisions is more likely to arrive at good decisions than a council where each member can attribute responsibility for mistakes to her colleagues. Committees are often accused of preferring easy caution to hard confrontation with a problem.

There is certainly a psychological problem here. It is easier to grasp and react to what an individual person intends than the amorphous intentions of a committee. One feels able to understand where the individual executive is coming from and what considerations influence her. To a serious degree this confidence is misplaced, easily exploited by leaders who have the knack of projecting the right image of themselves, exploit-ing the tropes of popular myths and platitudes, wishful thinking and paranoid fears. The dangers of the leadership principle are easily forgotten.

I believe that the objections to councils as committees can all be met if their workings are open to scrutiny and evaluation by anybody who is interested. This is now possible in ways that could hardly have been envisaged even a generation ago. The whole course of the deliberations of a council can now be recorded in full online, available for comment to anybody who is interested. Members of the council who have to advance clear arguments and engage with those of others in front of a critical public cannot hide behind anonymity or confidentiality. Their evasions and misconstruals of what is at issue are out in the open. One can have an assured confidence that the real issues are being addressed, that all and only the relevant considerations are being considered. Comments from the public are available at every point in the proceedings. The council is no longer a place where decisions are taken for covert reasons. The councillors are chosen by lot and are not beholden to supporters.

That assumes, of course, that discussion is not dominated by parties with preconceived positions, as in our parliaments, where what is said in debate on the floor of the house is often merely a staged confrontation on issues that have already been decided elsewhere. The difference between genuine debate in a context of negotiation and window-dressing is obvious. No council that claims to represent all the stakeholders could get away with a mere pretence of negotiation. A membership chosen by lot without precommitments or any debts to backers who enabled their candidatures can face the issues as they see them on their personal responsibility. The openings for power trading are minimal.

At the same time meetings need no longer take up too many fixed time slots. Debate can go on as members post submissions and replies on the website and read and respond to what others have to say when they get the time. In matters of policy, as distinct from execution, there is usually more scope to defer decision until the matter is thoroughly thrashed out. Members are able to look up relevant information or take expert advice before replying to points put to them. There is plenty of room for everybody to have their say unconstrained by the timetable of a meeting. It is often possible to express oneself more succinctly and precisely in writing than in speaking, and it is always easier to read and if necessary reread a text than to listen to a speech. If somebody insists on waffling, one doesn't have to listen patiently, but just cast an eye over it to assure oneself there is no substance to it.

Busy people can take an active role in the discussions without being tied down to inflexible timetables. It is an entirely different experience from that of dreary meetings. Of course it is desirable for councils to meet from time to time, preferably in informal contexts in which they can get to know each other better and learn more about their personal concerns.

The standing of demarchic councils is always going to depend almost entirely on their being seen to make good decisions. When it comes to a vote and the live alternatives have been adequately clarified, in many cases it will be a matter of choosing between closely comparable proposals. In such a case a simple majority may appropriately decide. In matters where it is clear that much greater risks are involved it may be wise to prolong the discussion in the hope of getting closer to consensus. It is the thoroughness of the discussion that must be evident in the verdict. Even if the council cannot reach a clear verdict, the result should be a clearer view of the issues raised in public discussion.

The major precedent for the use of sortition in current practice is the role of juries in the justice system. Many experiments in consulting public opinion have been described as 'citizen juries'. I want to emphasise the differences between the functions and procedures of the councils I advocate and the role of juries in the justice system. A basic difference is that jury service has to be compulsory. Most people do not want to be put in the position of condemning other people to punishment, and it is most undesirable that juries should be composed only of people who want to exercise such power. On the other hand, while many will find serving on a demarchic council onerous and disruptive to pursuits they value more highly, many people should find it attractive. It seems reasonable to assume that such people will want to be seen to do a good job, especially as their success in getting anything done depends entirely on the general perception of their performance.

Juries are obliged to follow the rules of evidence, basing their verdict solely on what is presented in court, and deciding guilt or innocence strictly according to the legal definition of the alleged crime. They are usually prohibited from discussing their deliberations outside of the jury room. That can be very frustrating where moral considerations and relevant factual knowledge would lead to a different verdict. By contrast, councils are entitled to consider anything they see as relevant to the problem they are addressing and are unconstrained by narrowly defined alternatives. They have the opportunity to make their case as their understanding of the wider public discussion develops. People who serve in a voluntary capacity on the councils are likely to at least make some claim to be capable of doing what they are required to do and to want to be seen to argue on grounds that are widely accepted as relevant.

Part Two

Suggested Solutions

Preliminaries

Summarising the conclusions of part one:

- Small councils are to be charged with the stimulation of public discussion on a specific practical policy problem.
- The initiative to set up such a body is open to any person or organisation that chooses to do so, but preferably would be the work of an independent foundation with experience in such work.
- The terms of reference and composition of the membership of the council would be decided by the agency that sets it up in the light of public discussion that suggests the need for such a body.
- In general the members of the decision-making council would be chosen by lot from a collection of individuals who are willing to serve and who between them are typical of those who are best equipped and motivated to give the issues serious consideration. In most cases the panel from which the council is chosen will be mainly ordinary people who are strongly and directly affected by the decisions in question. In others it will be a panel of people nominated by professional associations or other relevant sources as having the requisite expertise to judge the merits of proposals made to it. The panels will need to accept virtually unanimously the procedure by which the councils will be selected.
- The council's decisions would be guided by the need to convince public opinion that their conclusions are the best practical resolution of the various conflicting considera-

tions that emerge from public discussion of the issues. There is no claim that the procedures adopted by the council will be such that any other body is bound to accept them, but merely that they have a serious claim to being the best that can be done in the light of public debate on those issues.

- The proceedings of the council would be entirely public. The aim of their deliberations would be to arrive at an agreed conclusion, but the force of that conclusion would rest on the claims of the deliberation to thoroughness and fairness. Mere unanimity would not necessarily be convincing.
- It might be hoped that sometimes councils would succeed in going beyond the terms of current discussion and bring new light to bear on the problem it set out to address. The task is to get it right.
- Ultimately the policies the councils construct can be implemented only by the elected government, perhaps under pressure from voters who accept those conclusions as a fair set of judgements about the merits of the considerations advanced in the broader public discussion.

The following sketchy suggestions are intended to illustrate demarchic approaches to different kinds of problems. The underlying strategy is to establish procedures that come to be generally recognised as authoritative in their field of policy both by the various communities involved in that field and by other authorities. So the solutions they propose to the problems they address have a strong claim to be the best available solutions. There are plenty of important problems I do not address. A central concern is to show how we can have peaceful global order without anything like a global state, or even a federation of states such as the European Union. My strategy at the global level is in principle the same as at the domestic level, to confront existing authorities with the demand that they follow appropriately decided policies in certain specific matters where coordinated action is needed.

Global authorities of various sorts exist already, not to re-strict people's freedoms, but to provide frameworks in which it is possible for them to do things that would not otherwise be possible or possible only with much difficulty. There is already a surprising range of such authorities that we rarely have occasion to notice, regulating postal facilities, air traffic protocols, maritime safety, internet URLs, radio band-space, weather information and a host of other things. Apparently they mostly do a good job at reasonable cost, usually without anybody summoning them to account. Their clients are satisfied.

However, one cannot assume that good fortune will always hold. Every organisation tends to be run in the interests of those who have executive power in that organisation. Faced with several alternatives executives will naturally tend to take the one most congenial to themselves. An organisation tends to run most efficiently and smoothly where the interests of its executives and the interests of the organisation coincide. There are often entrenched practices that militate against such a desirable situation. The most obvious factor is the tendency of incumbents to turn their jobs into sinecures. So we may need to supervise them impartially.

These existing authorities do not provide an appropriate model for policy bodies to deal with the issues I am about to raise. Deciding what needs to be done to remedy certain problems in international finance or climate change or dis-armament calls for technical expertise to be deployed in the context of the often divergent social preferences of the people who make up the political agencies involved. Those differences call for negotiation between the people most affected by the problems at issue, rather than between the political communi-ties to which those people belong. What a supra-national body, as opposed to an international body, needs to do if it is to acquire sufficient authority to demand that states accept its directions is to show that it can take account of differing social situations in various countries without it being necessary for the states concerned to intervene. So the supra-national authority allocating targets for reducing carbon emissions in agriculture to various countries must show that they make due allowance for the differences between agricultural practices and communities in Bangladesh and Australia. Once the various states are involved in arriving at a scheme of responsibilities they will emphasise their differences and fail to find common ground. Confront them with a well-developed scheme and they can make a clear case for modifying it in some relevant respects.

In such a context it is vitally important that every relevant interest has an equal opportunity to make the case for its own needs and be assured that every effort will be made to meet them. But the body that makes the final decision about which allocations of responsibilities is the best and fairest plan cannot be based on an equal representation of every group that claims some legitimate interest in the matter. The most one can hope for, as with any jury, is to guard against too strong a bias in any of the obvious directions in the composition of the jury. The positive emphasis needs to be on the competence of the jury to survey all the relevant factors and arrive at a practical solution to the conflicts between them. An important advantage of removing any claim to institutionalised representation is that the fluid and diverse views of the various interests do not need to be solidified into a single position to which representatives are committed. All members of any group who have something to say can put their view forward for consideration on its merits. The sheer numbers of people who share a particular interest is always a consideration. But on a particular matter it may be much less important than the systemic significance of an activity. Not many people have a scientific interest in microbiology. But it is of great importance that microbiology be developed with a view to enlarging our knowledge and not just in pursuit of particular practical problems. Any scheme of representation has its inadequacies. Where the whole process of discussion takes place in public, not in some closed jury room, anybody who is interested is in a position at any stage to argue that their view has not been adequately considered. The council making the final decision has to justify its decision in response to such claims.

The best way of doing this in most cases will be for the council to draw up a suggested set of allocations of responsibilities and ask for comments on them. It then reconsiders various details in the light of the reasons people bring in favour of altering the balance between them and publishes a revised schedule for final comments. In the light of those comments it produces its final decision. This process allows each of the interests involved to negotiate with all the others taken collectively, something that is clearly necessary if they are to make a case for their interest in relation to all the others. It is only possible to argue that you have been unfairly treated if the overall result of the way others have been treated is clear and the reasons for all those decisions are out in the open. Your claim that you have been unfairly treated will only succeed if you can convince most other people that there are inconsistencies of a relevant kind between the way you have been treated and what has been done in the case of other interests.

No process of collective decision-making (or individual deliberation, for that matter) can guard against the possibility that the decision is seriously wrong. Perhaps in assessing various claims the council has tended to put too much trust in the validity of certain projections about the future, or it has given a lot of weight to economic considerations rather than to such social considerations as disrupting communities, and so on with every aspect of such a problems. Again, there is an ongoing problem of when to stick with an agreed decision in spite of growing doubts about it and when to reopen the whole question at the risk of paralysis and confusion. Continuity in policy is important. I would suggest that in a matter like this the council should be an ongoing body with the capacity to . make small changes to policy in the light of public discussion of various aspects of it. My suggestion is that the members of the council should serve for limited terms and be replaced by lot from the panel one or two at a time, avoiding the hazards of installing a complete team of inexperienced members who might too easily be persuaded to throw everything open for reconsideration.

Another theme in what follows is the need to break down complex problems into very specific ones. This is in direct contrast with the tendency to reject piecemeal solutions as incurably inadequate. I mention only a few of the many aspects of economic life that pose important problems. These are often attributed to a single source, namely capitalism. So nothing is of much use unless it gets rid of capitalism. In fact, capitalism is not just a parasitical growth on a free market, but its inevitable consequence. Production for trade between strangers in a competitive market inevitably depends on what exchanges are profitable in terms of money. In seeking to sell your product you don't need to find a buyer who has some particular thing you want, just someone who has money. Money is essential to generalised trading. Money can be stored and reinvested for further profit. Generalised trading is essential to enable people to exchange the particular things they have to sell for the variety of things they need. A world order based on self-sufficient communities trading by barter is no longer possible. Outside of such contexts as the family and very small communities people have to deal with each other on an impersonal basis. Exchange of goods and services in a competitive market must remain the normal mechanism of economic activity in any scenario we can envisage. What is possible is to tackle the problems of specific kinds of trading by very specific measures supervised by specialised authorities. The solution to the problems capitalism generates is not mass protests of the 'Occupy Wall Street' pattern, but constructive analysis and measured response to particular problems.

Suggestion one: The local scale

Despite the range of modern communications and organised production, much of our lives are still lived in localised networks and institutions. Local government remains crucial to the provision of most things we need in daily living. Just how local decisions on policy in these various matters need to be is always a question that depends partly on the history, geography, resources and aspirations of networks of people, and partly on the social and engineering technologies available to them. Different institutionalised needs will often be best served by authorities with different geographical boundaries. So water supply is dominated primarily by geographical factors. It usually needs to be developed on a much wider scale and with different emphasis than the provision of cultural or sporting facilities. Different policy considerations need to be considered.

It is, I think, not at all difficult to envisage the different ways in which demarchic councils might be set up, sometimes for a single decision, sometimes for an ongoing process of policy development, in response to the particular forms that problems take. It seems reasonable to hope that if such policy discussion occurred on a broad range of issues, it would have beneficial effects on the provision of public goods. The kind of considerations that need to be faced in planning a regional health service are clear. The question is whether we want to have them publicly decided or left to the professionals. In many ways local community interactions are declining as most of our supplies come from supermarkets and chain stores, our leisure activities range far and wide and families are scattered. Few people take an interest in local politics apart from on the occasions when they are adversely affected by some decision. Most decisions tend to be left to a relatively small group of people and mainly to various professional administrators, who mostly do a competent job. They avoid attracting attention to themselves. Apart from the occasional scandal, life goes on smoothly. I suggest we could do much better.

There is a fairly constant push to widen the geographical boundaries of local government bodies, allegedly in the interests of economies of scale, but also to weaken local chauvinism, which often stands in the way of the justified and unjustified ambitions of higher authorities. That expansion diminishes the significance of local interests in the political process and the motivation of people to participate actively if their focus is on very local matters. It opens the way to more far-reaching power trading than at a more local level, with the danger of worse corruption. There have been many instances all over the world of very successful episodic citizen committees at the local government level, but they have failed to become established as a regular feature of political activity, mainly, I think, because the stakes are not high enough for people to be driven to insist on them. The great benefits such decision-making might offer would be in raising the quality of local public goods, including a wide range of voluntary activities. How might this come about?

For most people at the height of their working lives the demands of work and family leave them with little energy to devote to activities that are not relaxing and pleasant. Serving on committees attempting to tackle contentious issues is not usually an attractive prospect for most of us. Quite a lot of people are willing to devote some time and money to supporting good causes or to fighting bad ones, but they find the attempt to master the range of considerations relevant to many problems too hard or too demanding. On the other hand we all do aspire to have control of our lives, at least in those aspects that we regard as important to our identities. To the extent that controlling those aspects of our lives has an intrinsic social dimension, we need to be assured that the processes by which the choices available to us are defined and assessed are likely to enrich rather than impoverish our lives.

We can have the sound assurance we need if we understand and trust those decision processes. That trust depends strongly on the general feeling in the community that the prevailing ways of arriving at policy decisions are appropriate and effective. The strength of that feeling will in turn depend on widespread experience of how they operate in practice and of the results they achieve. In such a context people can be expected to believe that it is in fact possible for them to participate in the decision process in some matters that they are concerned about with a reasonable hope of influencing the outcome and of gaining a better understanding of how their world works in the process. For the first time in history ordinary people would have direct experience of the processes by which social choices are made, coupled with the opportunity of participating actively in them. Many of them should find such participation interesting and challenging, particularly in matters that affect them directly and substantially. If that were to come about on a sufficient scale the result should be a society well educated in its self-understanding and well skilled in the art of negotiating conflicts of interest and aspiration. It is not just a question of the results we achieve, but of the sort of people we want to be. As I said in speaking of moralism, it is not that we all ought to be 'public spirited'. There are many other ways of leading an admirable life, but we do need enough people to be active in public life, just as we need artists and entrepreneurs.

A multi-faceted social pattern built up from particular decisions resembles the market in being able to claim some of its virtues of flexibility, sensitivity to demand and creating new demands. On the supply side, however, we have found the market favouring bigger productive organisations that can muster huge amounts of capital, exploit economies of scale and research and monopolise development. That involves highly centralised managements and decision-processes. Thinking in this pattern is equally attractive to providers of public goods, whether the providers are state institutions or large private operators. Similar claims are made for economies of scale, reliability of supply, incorporating best technology and efficient management. The large-scale private providers claim economic efficiency while the state organisations claim equity and political responsibility. Organisations strive to grow.

Accepting this tendency as irresistible is, I believe, increasingly anachronistic. The emerging patterns of our lives are much more complex and varied than either stereotype, megalopolis or village, can encompass. In education, health and many other activities that are coming to occupy more of our lives, the availability of appropriate information and its application in accordance with world standards is the central need in their proper functioning. On the one hand we need to shape our institutions to meet the particular needs of local people. On the other we need the guidance of experienced professionals in understanding and applying the relevant information to many situations. Even if we can understand the technical language and procedures it involves, applying any sound theory in practice always involves complications that cannot be deduced from the theory. Only professional experience can supply that need, just as only the people who need that assistance can assess whether it is meeting their needs. But it will often be the case that different public goods are best handled on a different local scale. Diversifying the institutions that provide them is now both possible and desirable. It may take more effort, but it should be worth it.

There are two kinds of local public goods that, I would suggest, more policy input and initiative from ordinary citizens might greatly improve, the feel of the environment and opportunities for cultural and sporting performances of all sorts. There are, of course, very many people who are employed by municipal authorities, especially in more affluent suburbs, who are very concerned to promote these things, but they lack active support, except where children are concerned. Then parents want their children to appreciate and participate in a host of activities that they have given up. In too many cases the children, as they grow up, are induced to regard many cultural and sporting activities as something to grow out of, unless they aspire to become star performers and appear on television. Perhaps if these activities were more actively governed by people with a particular interest in that particular kind of performance, more ways might emerge of stimulating interest in performance among adults. In regard to what I have called the feel of the environment, discussion is too frequently dominated by what affects real estate values. The issues are fought between developers and the owners of existing properties, usually on a very narrow set of considerations, profitability on the one hand and reluctance to have to face change on the other. A greater awareness of the distinctive role of public goods in our lives should come out of fuller public discussion of our preferences in regard to the environments.

If we are to maintain a high level of economic activity while reducing our impact on the ecosystem we will have to spend much less on hardware and much more on services, not on servants but on collaborations with professionals of all sorts in expanding our cognitive, social and aesthetic activities. Mass production will continue to have its place in supplying some of our basic needs reliably and cheaply (at the cost of trivialising them to a great extent), but the things that define us as persons in our interactions with the world and in our personal relationships need to grow subtler, more variously expressive and inevitably more expensive in terms of our own time and that of others. The particular forms this growth takes are unpredictable, but it will inevitably involve social decisions, some of which will need to be taken deliberatively.

The quality of the relationship between professionals and those who need their advice is probably the key element in such matters as education and health care. Constructing arrangements that foster a sense of personal responsibility on the one side and trust on the other is a multidimensional problem. Certification, defining standards and providing opportunities and incentives to update the knowledge of professionals need decisions on a large scale. But interesting people in improving their own understanding and perspectives calls for arrangements that involve all parties together in achieving the best results possible in the circumstances. Raising pupils' sights from concentrating on high marks in certain exams to an appreciation of the joys of learning, moving patients away from obsessions with medication to a healthy lifestyle and similar desirable objectives are not likely to be achieved if what the carer does is merely to go through a routine prescribed by bureaucratic regulations. The best improvements in what is actually done are to be expected where those concerned at the level of final delivery services have as much input into their arrangements as possible. How that is to be done must be a matter for experiment at that level.

That has its costs, but the demand that public goods be as cheaply funded as possible must be resisted.

Assuming that a local health or educational authority is assigned a budget from centralised tax revenues on something like a per capita basis, it will often be the case that the cost of any really satisfactory scheme to meet some particular community's needs will exceed that budget. If people identify with the organisation and have confidence in its value for money, they will normally be quite prepared to pay for it. That can easily be arranged by a surcharge on local land taxes and on the income tax paid by those who are entitled to use the facilities in question. The needs of a struggling community may also attract philanthropic support. Donors who hate to finance the promises of politicians may be much more sympathetic to a community project. Often the difference between the cost of a good service and a poor one can be quite small in relation to total taxation. The main difficulty is to avoid organising these structures on an overly parochial scale that enables the rich to provide themselves with excellent schools and hospitals and leaves the poor with inadequate provision.

The councils charged with planning such organisations need to be representative of the stakeholders, both the final providers and particular consumers. They are dependent on each other to make best use of the resources available in the light of the specific needs they serve. The best way of achieving such representation is to choose the representatives by a statistical procedure from those who are willing to serve on the council in question. Granted an appropriate analysis of the relative importance of the various interests involved, it should not be difficult to get an agreement on how to set up a selection procedure that is acceptable to the stakeholders. Many candidates will have several distinct interests, not just as particular sorts of both consumers and producers, but as involved in family and other responsibilities. They can be scored along these different dimensions in the selection process. There is no need for them to be identified as representing one interest as opposed to others. In a negotiating process people who have a problem of reconciling the impact of conflicting interests in their own case can often be very useful in evolving ways of bringing those interests into harmony.

There is, however, no ideal way of designing such a scheme of representation or of setting it up on a scale that avoids parochialism and captures economies of scale without being too remote from its clients. Obviously, it is a matter of trial and error. One has to start by building on existing structures and improving them in the light of experience and critical evaluation of their fairness. My suggestion is that in the case of ongoing councils steady improvement could be achieved if changes were the result of interested groups arguing for changes they see as needed before an impartial body with power to change the formulae on which representation was based and the scope of the organisation's coverage. Such reviewing authorities would be constituted by lot from a pool of candidates nominated by their peers on the basis of their service on representative bodies as having the qualities required for doing a good job at the higher level. Everything proceeds from the bottom upwards, not from the top down and in the light of the needs of the job, not power politics.

Such experiments could be introduced into existing institutions as a matter of administrative restructuring in the light of particular problems in certain areas, not as some grandiose plan imposed from above. My hope would be that it would be seen to work well and spread rapidly, adapting to different situations in flexible forms. Existing legislative structures and much top administrative structure would remain intact, but their importance would diminish gradually because so many matters of substance would be decided at the 'lower' levels. It is not at all difficult to envisage how the delivery of consumer services in such matters as health, education and support for the needy might be arranged. In time we might discover better ways of handling law and order than our present adversarial procedures for making and administering the law. But that is for the future. I have concentrated on ways in which demarchic procedures could be introduced without prior political agreement or legislative changes.

There are also many matters that are sources of corruption in our present structures, such as building permits, the issuing of mining licences and other decisions that give special advantages to certain interests. It is not difficult to see how councils chosen by an appropriate statistical procedure could reduce the possibility of corruption in such matters. That could involve legislative changes, which in turn would depend on such procedures having achieved general acceptance.

Suggestion two: The national scale

The aim of my proposals is not to introduce any change in the institutions of contemporary democracies but to institute a practice of deriving from public discussion a practical policy that politicians would have to take seriously as what the voters expect of them. At present policy is too often sacrificed to the power struggles of politicians. To illustrate my point I adduce a single episode in Australian politics. Naturally it bears the marks of the peculiar situation in which it happened, but the kind of factors involved and the effects they have can easily be seen at work in many other countries and situations.

In July 2007 John Howard, prime minister in the coalition conservative government seeking re-election, promised to introduce an Emissions Trading Scheme (ETS), as did his opponent, Labor leader, Kevin Rudd. Rudd, who was personally very popular, was elected. Howard had lost his seat in parliament and was replaced as leader of the Liberal-National coalition by Malcolm Turnbull, who also favoured an ETS. Rudd was an enthusiastic advocate of action on climate change, but left the introduction of an ETS until after the Copenhagen conference on climate change, which he hoped might provide a basis for international action.

In November 2009 Rudd negotiated with Turnbull a broad agreement about the first steps on the path to an ETS, but on December 1 the Liberals, after an internal power struggle won by a single vote, replaced Turnbull with the less popular but more combative Tony Abbott, who immediately announced his rejection of an ETS. Meanwhile the Copenhagen conference failed dismally. Although the Labor party remained committed to an ETS, the option that enjoyed the almost unanimous support of expert opinion, Rudd decided to delay its implementation until the international position was clearer.

In June 2010, again because of internal strife in the party, the popular Rudd was replaced as PM by Julia Gillard, who called an election to legitimise her position in the eyes of the electorate. In the course of the election campaign she explicitly promised not to introduce a carbon tax, as proposed by the Greens. When the election results delivered her more seats than the coalition, but not a majority in the House of Representatives, she needed the support of the Greens to govern. They made it a condition of that support that she introduce a carbon tax. So in November 2011 she legislated a carbon tax. The coalition insisted that she had not only broken her promise, but that the carbon tax would be 'a tax on everything' that would be passed on to all consumers indiscriminately.

In June 2013, facing the probability of electoral defeat, the Labor party demoted Gillard and reinstated Rudd, who immediately announced that he would repeal the carbon tax. He lost the subsequent election to Abbott. After much politicking in the Senate, the tax was finally removed in July 2014 and replaced by the coalition policy of subsidising firms to adopt more carbon-efficient technologies, a dubiously effective solution that had to be financed from taxation, but not from a special tax. There was fairly general agreement that it was not a good policy, but Abbott was wedded to his policy. Turnbull finally replaced Abbott in September 2015, but deferred a reconsideration of his policy.

If there had been a clear expression of public opinion on the matter, there can be little doubt that both parties would remain committed to an ETS, but public debate remained tributary to the focus on party politics rather than the issue itself. In fact during her election campaign Gillard had floated the idea of summoning a formal citizen's convention to debate and decide on the issue if she was elected, but the suggestion was general-ly dismissed as evading her responsibility and she did not persevere with it. If we are to break free from the grip of party politics the initiative for and structure of policy committees has to come from outside that arena. The particular shape of the council in a particular matter needs to be determined in view of the range and character of the issues it addresses. Once again, what is paramount is getting a vigorous public discussion and a jury that is well equipped to derive a practical policy from it.

The issue of what to do about carbon emissions is a good example of the difficulties of relying on representation, whether of people or of interests, to validate the results of a decision process, instead of looking at the arguments and evidence advanced in favour of its conclusion. For example, all consum-ers, whether households or industries, share a common interest in cheap electricity, but it affects them in very different ways. Many consumers regard it as a point in favour of a carbon tax that it imposes costs on households, because they typically waste a lot of energy and need to be prodded into changing their ways. It is unfortunate that more frugal consumers, including themselves presumably, will also be affected. In fact in Australia raising the price of electricity did have that result, affecting adversely the recently privatised suppliers, who assumed demand would continue to rise. What really matters is not whether this or that interest is represented on the council, but whether the different considerations that affect those people are properly taken into account. Public opinion needs to be convinced of that. If some group claims it has not been given due consideration, it needs to argue that the result really is unfair to it in some specific consequences.

The story also illustrates the importance of developing inter-national public opinion on many matters, in order to take the task of constructing a world policy on those issues out of the distorting focus of national politics. In the absence of an international view of the matter, countries come to a negotia-tion primarily concentrating on not sacrificing their own interests to those of their competitors. Even what can be achieved in domestic politics is often dependent on how people think the rest of the world sees them in the context. I have already explained the importance of having at least a preliminary allocation of responsibilities before a nation can be in a position to decide on its position in regard to them.

Suggestion three: Security

The supreme concern of tribes, nations and states is still war, or, more euphemistically, defence or national security. We now know very well that war is almost always irrational, even from the viewpoint of the aggressor. Wars waged on the classic pretexts, dynastic aggrandisement, the control of natural resources, the imposition of true religion and the liberation of the oppressed have, each in different ways, proved to be both costly and futile. It is very much cheaper and less dangerous to buy natural resources on the market than to attempt to 'mine them with bayonets'. A religion that can gain adherents only by force devalues its claim to truth and supernatural power. Even the liberation of the oppressed almost inevitably takes on the aspect of imposing an imported system of authority in the interests of the 'liberator'. The glory of military heroics fades to nothing compared to the suffering war inflicts on people.

War is a contagious disease. If, in spite of its horrors we have not developed adequate anti-bodies or vaccines for it, I believe the reason is not just that recourse to violence is so attractive to us. It offers the specious prospect of destroying evil. Heroism is always appealing to some young men, and much of our literature and our traditions glorify it. More fundamentally, people have been convinced that the supreme test of a nation's worth is its capacity to act in unison, facing death rather than surrender, sinking doubts in loyalty. In a more constructive and sensitive moral perspective, the greater test of the moral worth of a nation would be to meet violence with steady and persistent resistance to its demands. Gandhi was the greatest political hero of his age. Nevertheless, the idea that war is a legitimate instrument of policy survives, legitimised by the celebration of good wars.

When Britain undertook to crush the revolt of the American colonies, many significant voices in Britain itself saw the stupidity of it, but outright opposition was out of the question. Once war is declared, opposition is treason and treason is the ultimate political crime. Britain, fortunately for its other settler colonies, learned its lesson, but it left a bad inheritance to the United States. When the USA itself was faced with the secession of the Southern States, instead of accepting their decision, the North undertook to suppress it. Lincoln's reason for doing so was beautifully expressed in the Gettysburg Address. He was concerned that if the United States could not show the world that it could preserve its unity, democracy would be completely discredited and 'perish from the earth'. Not only was he almost certainly wrong about that, he allowed American prestige as the home of democracy to endorse the prejudice of the old regimes of Europe that the state has the right and the duty to suppress secession at all costs. The determination of the moribund Austrian dynasty to maintain its Balkan empire in the face of nationalist demands for independence led to the Great War, which in turn led to the horrors of Hitler and Stalin.

If the South had been allowed to secede it would have had to face the unanimous rejection of slavery by the rest of the world and find its own way out of its predicament. Almost certainly the results for race relations in America would have been happier than the present situation. Americans might have been much more critical of the use of force to suppress bad regimes instead of exploring peaceful but powerful alternatives. Once the context of war is removed, regimes have at least to pretend to offer a good life to their subjects. Tyrannies thrive on paranoia. The moral and economic requirements of a decent human life in the modern world cannot be fudged in the era of global communications. Cultural contact can change things for the better rapidly and effectively. The experience of attempting to solve social problems by destroying bad regimes neglects the fundamental point that fruitful change in any society depends on its actively developing forms of self-organisation that can handle its problems effectively without violence.

Patience is indispensible. It is not so long ago that most of Latin America and many other countries were military dictatorships. In nearly all those instances the dictatorships failed, mainly because they could not handle the problems of meeting the needs of a modern society. The democratic regimes that have replaced them have suffered from the absence over so many decades of a vigorous and realistic civil society, as well as from the inherent defects of populist democracy. But there is no going back to dictatorship. The old claim that autocracy is effective and efficient is unsustainable in the contemporary world.

We are only slowly coming to recognise that our most urgent problems need to be addressed from a global perspective. But they must not be bundled together. The UN is not the answer to most problems of international order. The structure of the United Nations is doubly defective. Its membership consists of states, not people. So its first defect is that it fails to give proper consideration to those interests that people have that transcend the perspectives of states. Many actions are excluded because states see them as increasing the power of the UN at the expense of their own. The second defect is that the UN works by power-trading between states that treat people's needs primarily as pawns in the game of maximising their own power.

Treating all the issues that we face at a supranational level as if they were merely problems of relations between nation states is to misconstrue them. The dangers of climate change arise out of the international economic system. They are not reducible to the activities of states. The ability of any state to act effectively on the problem depends on the problem being addressed from a global perspective. As long as the decision about what needs to be done is primarily a matter of the internal politics of each state and power struggles between states—any attempts to get effective agreement about how to deal with global warming are doomed to fail in a welter of faked agreement and mutual recriminations. At both national and global levels the solution is to put policy on specific matters in the hands of those who are most competent and strongly motivated to get it right.

Most of our global problems are unprecedented. Finding effective ways of handling them is important and urgent, not just because of the direct effects attendant on failing to deal with them effectively, but because failure is likely to lead to violent conflict that will make things much worse. If we fail in meeting our most challenging needs for coordinated action, as the global situation deteriorates people will despair of reason and fall back on arbitrary power.

The most prominent threats to peace in the contemporary world are ideological. But it is simply absurd to think we can oppose them effectively by force. They flourish on totalising enmity. Ideologues subordinate all other considerations to imposing an exclusive regime on some community by seizing state power. They are resistant to rational criticism. We have to rely on undercutting their economic and practical bases, mainly by indirect action—in the economic case by such tactics as stifling their trade and in practice by presenting the attractions of a different way of life, not as some competing ideology, but as a complex of sensible ways of dealing with practical problems that people face. In the long run ideologies are self-destructive. They cannot live up to their own pretentions. They may be effective in mobilising activity, but it is always mis-directed.

The only secure basis for the security of each and every nation is a world order in which the good functioning of all the collective activities we need together is assured by appropriate regulation of each of them. The crucial thing is to stop decisions from being pawns in power struggles, however well-intentioned. Such an order does not demand unanimity on everything that is important. We have to get used to accepting decisions we don't agree with and tolerating a certain amount of deviance. The rest of the world can put up with the oddities of American exceptionalism when it comes to weights and measures, or even to the International Court of Justice. What is not sustainable is any conception of a world order resting upon the decisions of a single power exercising an overwhelming military superiority. It has proved itself incapable of keeping the peace, let alone dealing with the sources of conflict.

The strongest contribution the economically developed democracies can make to the political maturation of the undeveloped countries is to embrace the process of instituting genuinely supranational authorities that are clearly not just tools of their privileged power. In that way it may become apparent that authority need not be the expression of some mythical unity, but a means of facilitating experiment in dealing with our problems. Global authorities must address global problems from a global perspective and tackle the specific causes of that particular problem. To take an obvious instance, the many problems of regulating the use of the seas and of space take us beyond the traditional order based on territorial powers and their interests. We need to start with specific problems, such as the preservation of marine species, building a supranational order out of particular practical decisions.

Many diagnoses of our economic problems and their social consequences place the blame on capitalism. That is not a practical approach. Capitalism is the inevitable pattern of an unfettered market economy. The only comprehensive alternative is to organise all production and distribution by a state bureaucracy. That is both oppressive and inefficient. But we are not confined to a choice between two totalising alternatives. We have many choices of ways of combining exchange and rationing in developing solutions to particular problems. There is no single right way of handling all economic problems. Markets are not closed systems. We can and must intervene in them, but with as good an understanding as we can get of what we are doing. We can hardly avoid intervening in some genetic processes, but the importance of good decisions about such matters can hardly be exaggerated.

Our choices are not simple. We do insist that governments should pay appropriate attention to particular matters of policy. But our present means of giving force to that insistence are inadequate to the task. On the international scale there is no hope of achieving the sort of unity that is possible at the national level. The problems are too complex. Allowing the whole range of our global issues to be decided by whoever wields most power is a recipe for disaster. It is urgent that we develop a range of independent authorities whose authority is simply a matter of their supplying competent guidance to the various agents who need to be regulated or coordinated. Their power must rest on peoples and institutions insisting that their guidance be accepted. Power always rests on two pillars, organisation and incentives to do what it requires. A viable international order is not something that can be designed from a plan. It is an intricately complex and uncontrollable eco-system. We may be able to intervene effectively where the ecosystem is in danger from internal imbalances or external factors, but only if we can break down the task into managea-ble projects.

One crucial practical problem is disarmament. The only hope of stopping arms races lies in establishing an independent body with capacity to get its decisions accepted by organising peaceful sanctions. Clearly it must proceed gradually. It is often best to start with the least important problems and work up to the more important ones. Or it may be more effective to begin with newly emergent problems where novel measures may be more readily accepted. Other crucially important problems, such as population growth, can only be addressed indirectly. An international one-child policy is inconceivable. Similarly, the economic problems we face as the pressure on essential resources builds up can never be reduced to some programme of redistribution of assets. People will be convinced that war and threats of war solve nothing only when they see that other means of getting things done are effective and available.

Suggestion four: International finance

Until the wartime Bretton Woods agreement was abandoned in the early 1970s each state had a great deal of control over its own financial system. States could fix the exchange rate of their currency against other currencies and control imports and exports of capital. Since these controls were abolished there has been an exponential growth of the global market in money, as distinct from the other goods, the commodities and services that money can buy. It is said that the volume of trade in money is as much as forty times the aggregate of all other items of trade put together. Nearly all that trading is entirely divorced from any particular lending for production or consumption. It is principally a matter of seizing on temporary discrepancies between the prices of a currency in different markets, buying a particular currency where it is cheap and selling it where it is dearer. There is a good deal to be said in favour of allowing the market to determine the relative values of currencies, but not if that trading adversely affects trade in commodities and services.

Unrestricted money trading is a form of gambling that imposes costs on other trade. The price of many currencies falls precipitately as traders try to get rid of them in anticipation of further falls, while prices rise equally rapidly in the opposite circumstances. Buyers and sellers of commodities who need to be able to buy or sell at a predictable price often have to buy futures, agreements with agents to supply their requirements at a fixed price at some future date. If offering futures is to be profitable it must in the long run impose a significant cost on the trade, making trading more expensive than if exchange rates were more stable. The firms that sell currency futures are usually the same as those that speculate on the money market.

This trading has become so profitable because of almost instantaneous communication of information, split second response and equally rapid transmission of payments. Computers collect and process the requisite information, respond in accordance with a sophisticated program and complete the transaction in microseconds. The human role is reduced to keeping an eye on the way the trading is developing. The transaction costs are minimal and the buying and selling is completed so quickly that the capital is back where it started from almost immediately, ready for another excursion to anywhere in the world. The discrepancies that this trading exploits are usually very small, but the trading is very profitable because the capital can be turned over so many times in a single day as often as a discrepancy shows up.

There is a lot of serious support for the view that such trading needs at least to be curtailed. I am inclined to think that it may be an important mechanism working towards the present surge in the concentration of wealth, along with the boom in the price of assets such as real estate. It allows money to make money without investing in anything that improves the supply of what we really need. There is a simple way of curtailing it. Impose a small tax on exchanges of currencies. The discrepancies that the trading exploits are usually quite small. A small tax on every trade could make most of them unprofitable. No country can impose such a tax unilaterally without disadvantaging its own financial institutions. It seems clear that this and other problems in international finance can only be dealt with by an international authority that monitors and responds to them on a regular basis, deploying on a global scale some of the functions that reserve banks perform at the national level. The existing authorities, the International Monetary Fund and the World Bank were designed in the context of the defunct Bretton Woods agreements and the politics of the immediate post-war era. They have notorious deficiencies.

Perhaps an authority that could remedy some of these problems might be set up on the initiative of a group of reserve banks. In practice, just as a national economy needs an authority that regulates money supply in its currency so as to ensure price stability, it seems desirable that there be a single stable international currency in which prices of important commodities could be reliably expressed, independently of fluctuations in the values of particular currencies. At Bretton Woods Keynes proposed creating such a currency, regulated by an independent authority. His proposal was rejected and the US dollar was installed in that role. Eventually the United States decided not to continue to observe some of the undertakings it agreed to at Bretton Woods, notably to tie the dollar to gold. But it still continues to serve as the world currency because of its economic power. The prices of most commodities and most international debts are expressed in dollars. As the size of the Chinese economy grows to rival that of the US, it is now seeking to acquire a similar status for its currency. That makes the question of a genuine reserve currency much more urgent.

Reserve banks in most advanced countries now have a great deal of independence in making decisions in matters that not so long ago were political decisions, such as interest rates and the quantity of money in circulation. They began as administrative offices. In time politicians turned to them for advice. Faced with unpopular decisions the politicians pleaded that they were following the non-political advice of the reserve bank. Eventually they decided to offload the full responsibility for such decisions on to the bank. It is an excellent example of how so many kinds of decisions about specific matters of quite general importance in many other connections turn out to be best taken by people whose immediate focus is on the specific needs of the particular institution or functions they are meant to serve. It would be much better if such institutions were composed of members reflecting the interests of all those affected by the decisions taken.

It is irrational that we entrust the task of providing a reliable international currency to particular states whose behaviour is governed by domestic considerations and their attempts to dominate others. Once again I would suggest the procedure of the parties most affected nominating suitable people to a pool of experts from which a directorate would be chosen by lot, in order to ensure that the directors are not beholden to any political interests. It would be rational for national authorities to accept such an authority; since in most respects it would not restrict them in anything they need to do, while the increased stability and predictability of money markets would be useful to them.

Suggestion five: Climate change

Note: The following section was written some years ago as a response to several distinguished scientist friends, not climate specialists, who professed themselves unconvinced by the evidence on which the IPCC (International Panel on Climate Change) based its claims. So the first part of it is probably no longer applicable. I have let it stand because it is an example of a way of proceeding that may have applications in other contexts.

Global action on the problem of human-induced climate change is stalled. In most countries action has become a victim of internal politics as well as of the absence of any international authority capable of organising a concerted response. Everybody waits for others to do something. The politics involved in the workings of the UN prevent it from providing a solution to the absence of an international authority, and attempts to get one set up by treaty seem hopeless. That suits a lot of vested interests.

In this situation even the scientific authority of the IPCC has come into question. It is alleged to be biased and complicit in the attempts of certain professional and political interests to exploit fear of catastrophe. Also it is not effectively answerable to anybody. There is obviously not just some plausibility but some substance to these accusations. There is no doubt that everybody who works for the IPCC is already convinced that climate change is dangerous and that it is at least exacerbated by our use of fossil fuels. They want to find more evidence for their view. They may be nominally responsible to the UN, but in practice that is a formality. Like any institution, the UN tends to expand its own power.

In this situation it is easy for those who oppose the IPCC to make accusations that sound very plausible to those who are unable to evaluate the accusations for themselves. What is clearly needed is an impartial body that can encourage specific, well-argued accusations against the IPCC and evaluate them in a publicly accessible and impartial way. The fact that members of the IPCC are committed does not imply that they will only attend to data that suit their views or draw unwarranted conclusions. In fact, if they are confident in their conclusions they will normally be motivated to make sure that they do not leave themselves open to such accusations. Nevertheless, such accusations need to be examined publicly, competently, impartially, authoritatively and in detail. How is it possible to constitute the appropriate body?

Let a consortium of major foundations agree to finance it for a specific period and set up a steering committee to secure the cooperation of the IPCC and of major universities throughout the world. The steering committee will call on each of those universities to nominate one or two people who are not involved professionally or publicly with questions of climate change, but possess the sort of abilities necessary to understand the scientific issues involved. That will produce a panel of perhaps two hundred. The actual jury will consist of ten or a dozen members chosen by lot from the panel, subject to appropriate constraints, such as that no jury contain more than one citizen of any one country.

The jury will be appointed to examine a particular case, which has been deemed by the panel as meriting investigation. It will not aim at a simple 'guilty/not guilty' verdict or at unanimity. Rather each juror will be asked, in relation to each specific aspect of the evidence produced, to assess any probability that the evidence might warrant the accusation of scientific malpractice, say on a scale of 0-10, and to comment on their reasons for that assessment. The jury might proceed to produce an agreed assessment by a process like that used in scoring performances in sports such as gymnastics, diving and figure skating. Scores that deviate so far from the median as to be idiosyncratic are dropped and an average is taken of the rest. In many cases that might come out as zero, but in such complex and disputable material, it would not be damning to be given a score of one or two. People have genuine differences about the weight to be given to a piece of evidence. In any case the point of the exercise would not be in the verdict so much as in what emerged in the process of arriving at it.

It might well be that small groups of dissident scientists who think they have a serious case against the consensus will feel that the whole arrangement is just a move to discredit them unheard. They lack the resources to mount the sort of case that demands to be taken seriously. It might be necessary to assure them that if they can convince the panel that they have a case that should be heard, they will receive adequate financial support to mount it before the tribunal. It is likely that the major vested interests that want to discredit the IPCC will decide that their best tactic is to ignore the panel or prevent it from getting any sort of recognition. So they will not fund any challenge. Dissident scientists might also be wary of accepting overt funding from vested interests as it could undermine the perceived validity of their case.

Granted that such accountability led to a well-grounded consensus about the need for concerted and adequate action on a global scale, it would be necessary to face the question how could such action be organised? I suggest that the scientific panel might establish another panel to assign responsibilities to particular agents, multi-nationals and especially states. That panel would need to involve much broader expertise than the scientific panel itself. It would delegate to particular councils the detailed decisions that need to be made. At every stage the operating procedures of these bodies would be open to scrutiny by interested opinion. They would need to acquire a status that would put most other relevant authorities under strong pressure to accept them because of the clear need for immediate and effectively coordinated action. I doubt whether the United Nations General Assembly could handle the problem effectively. It is too politicised and would bring a host of irrelevant considerations into the matter. It might well have a role in setting up an independent body. The authority of such an independent body would depend on its being seen as designed to deal appropriately with the particular task of getting a sufficient measure of agreement on the responsibilities of the agencies whose cooperation is needed.

That body might initiate its work by setting overall targets and attempting to assign particular targets to particular agencies in the light of their past contribution to warming and their capacity to contribute to averting further damage. Each agency would have the opportunity of disputing its allocation on such grounds as the weight of the burden their allocation would place on it as compared to the burden on other agencies.

I think that it is clear that such an approach would be more likely to produce a satisfactory overall response than direct negotiations between the various agencies. What happens when all the countries of the world come together to frame an agreement on their responsibilities is that they attempt to find a simple formula that applies to all, with perhaps some agreed provision for special cases. If this target is set so as to be acceptable to nearly all, it is very likely to be too low. In many cases there may be good reason in terms of their particular situation for wanting more differentiated targets. But there is no way for each agency to argue its special case with all of the others. It would dissolve into a mess of vicious circles. If one agency attempts to take the lead, setting a high target and challenging others to follow it, there will always be a host of political reasons for many others to refuse to follow. There can be no substitute for a body that assigns the burdens in the light of the best scientific estimates of what is needed and the capacity of each contributor to the problem to contribute to its solution.

Such a body would involve quite different expertise and a very different modus operandi from the jury on the IPCC. Its task involves practical negotiations. I think that it would still need to be based on selecting the membership of the decision-making body by lot from a relatively large group of nominees. The point would be to give every body affected by the scheme an opportunity to have an input into setting it up, but getting down to a realistic number those actually doing the work. These matters have to be decided in relation to their particular historical circumstances. The group of nominees could retain some supervisory role over the decision-making body.

For such a scheme to work it is necessary that most of the parties involved be prepared to give it at least a provisional acceptance and to be able to rely on the public to which they are responsible being prepared to accept it as at least worth a trial. Perhaps they can be induced to consider it if they realise that this is a case where if everybody attempts to pursue their own interests in opposition to all the others, that will inevitably lead to the worst result for everybody. If those who go along with the authority include the major actors, the authority will eventually find ways of shaming the rest into at least pretence of compliance.

Suggestion six: Auditing

Over the past twenty-five years the idea of auditing has been extended far beyond financial contexts to cover such various matters as the performance of researchers, teachers, police, medical procedures, environmental policies and countless other activities. It is often applied with pseudo-rigorous exactitude, neglecting the indeterminacies, absence of appropriate metrics and the specifics of different problems. Moreover, an auditing procedure inevitably shapes the activities to which it is applied, often inappropriately, when the requirements of rigid methodologies override the requirements of the task being audited. Anxiety to avoid blame may lead to a stifling preference for safe choices. There is no substitute for trust in most practical matters. Judgements about timing of action, assessment of risks, the scope of opportunities and relevant externalities are central to action. Such exercises of judgement can be fully assessed only retrospectively, often in the light of knowledge not available at the time the decision was taken. In planning and acting we have to trust people to make responsible guesses.

As I argued earlier, an audit framed as a simplified cost–benefit exercise may be useful in keeping an eye on certain factors, but not as a substitute for more ample and flexible assessments, even from a narrowly economic point of view. It is striking that so many of the business conglomerates of a generation ago have disappeared and many large corporations have been divesting themselves of non-core operations. They have found that sophisticated financial management is no substitute for the sort of understanding of the specifics of a particular kind of operation that comes only from experience in the processes of producing and marketing the relevant products in a given situation. 'Bean-counting' is never an adequate guide to good policy.

Over the past twenty years there has been great stress placed on governance of corporations of all sorts. One very welcome aspect of this has been a focus on accountability and a demand that the interests of all stakeholders (including the environment), not just shareholders, be taken into account. Much discussion and activity has been directed towards forms of auditing that record not just the financial position of the corporation, but also the effects of its operations on many other interests. The assumption has been that managers will be forced to recognise their responsibilities for the effects of their decisions on people and the planet, as well as profit. There is no doubt that some investors and managements have aspired to meet these demands. Many others have taken refuge in what the law allows. Laws rarely do more than penalise the more egregious forms of damage to people and the environment.

What audits can do falls short of what people expect from them. They are just inevitably summary reports. They can reveal that something is going wrong, but not how to deal with it. If the information an audit summarises is inadequate or poorly recorded and processed it may offer no basis for understanding why things have gone wrong. That is difficult enough in strictly financial matters. It becomes incomparably more difficult when very different considerations are brought into the enquiry. Many efforts have been made to find ways of assigning monetary values to effects on people and the planet. In some cases it is not too difficult to assign damages to a particular action. Often things are much too complex for that to be possible. Where we can identify a clear danger of such consequences we usually deal with it by prohibitions when what is most needed are incentives to adopt an appropriate attitude to the considerations in question.

Prohibition is often difficult to manage when certain things that are harmless on a small scale, say burning fossil fuel, pose enormous problems on a larger scale. We can't simply prohibit their use. The only practical way of cutting it down is to make it more expensive. The incentive to reduce consumption feeds directly into financial decisions, making other sources of energy more attractive, stimulating research into greater efficiency and so on. Above all, it has its effect on every user of fossil fuel in proportion to their use of them. In theory that is just; in practice the poor need to be compensated for the disproportionate burden it places on them. The political problems are notorious. It is hard to persuade people to vote for increased taxes. If the amount of the tax and the compensations to be made were set by a demarchic council with no political agenda. all major parties might prefer to agree on its verdict, rather than be caught in a race to the bottom. As with so many economic measures that are necessitated by global problems, the only fully satisfactory arrangement is for such a tax to be levied worldwide, taking account of differences in capacity to pay. Some payment for the enduring effects of past use of fuels seems required by justice where it continues to affect the present situation.

The positive role of auditing is to encourage good behaviour by disseminating an appropriate assessment of the degree to which the institutions examined live up to their own pretentions. That is an adequate orientation only when the pretentions of the institution are appropriate to its social significance. It is not enough for a firm to claim that its only obligation is to maximise the return to its shareholders. But that is all that traditional auditing monitors. Any firm that values long-term success strives to be seen as trustworthy and sensitive to what is expected of it. The most effective way of regulating the policies and practices they adopt is by making clear what is expected of them and insisting on knowing how well they have lived up to those expectations. It is necessary for there to be processes that set clear standards of conduct and produce clear assessments of a firm's behaviour. Legislation is usually too inflexible for this role. Firms need to be punished for telling lies, and the punishment needs to be sheeted home to the individuals who are responsible for those corporate lies or even, perhaps, for failing to reveal them. Targeting people's behaviour is usually fairer and more effective than punishing them for the results of what they do, because it makes allowance for genuine mistakes and unforeseen factors.

Auditing as we know it had its origin in the need of owners to check on the behaviour of their employees, to see that all payments and receipts were accounted for. It was then developed to give the entrepreneur a clear picture of the financial position of the firm and then to give investors that sort of information. In order to protect the interests of investors and of the wider public, regulations were introduced specifying what information the audit was required to supply. Such requirements make for a conflict of interest in the role of the auditor. As an agency under contract to the firm's directorate it is bound to promote their interests. As an agency charged with certifying publicly that certain information about the firm's financial position is correct, it is bound to do so in the interests of investors. But often the interest of the firm is to conceal certain liabilities or risks that, once acknowledged, might destroy its capacity to borrow the money it needed or to attract investors. Such situations are often not simple. The disclosure in question may be exaggerated by certain pundits in a way that will destroy the firm. On the other hand, if the disclosures are not made the firm may succeed in honouring its commitments and covering its risks. There are powerful incentives for firms to adopt forms of partial disclosure that are not strictly honest but may well pass as complying with the strict letter of the relevant regulations.

This kind of situation is rapidly becoming more prevalent as huge amounts of money are under the management of trustee funds and investment funds of all sorts. Investing in stocks and bonds is necessarily a gamble. The funds enable people to invest their savings more safely by spreading the risk over many investments. Increasingly that gambling in investments takes place in a very short perspective. It is a matter of predicting short-term market rises or falls and buying and selling accordingly. Cash flow is all-important. Most investment funds have no interest in the long-term success of any firm they invest in, but only in the next movement in its market price. Such trading is increasingly divorced from the realities of production and consumption. It is a matter of turning over one's investments as frequently as an opportunity to realise a gain offers itself.

Commercial rating agencies that purport to inform investors about the risks in various investments cannot be trusted. Conflicts of interest are inherent in their operations. In the context of present patterns of investment, they favour the short term over the long term in unsustainable ways. They may know that the investment they recommend as likely to rise in price tomorrow is bound to crash in the longer term and that the more that is invested in it the sooner that term is likely to arrive. All that matters is whether it will arrive before tomorrow, when their clients have taken their capital gain and moved on. Their certifying as risk-free very risky assets was central to the collapse of 2008, but they went unpunished and are still in business, their judgement still being heeded for lack of anything better. They are the astrologers of finance.

What the social and ecological effects of this situation are in the longer term, and what can be done about them are matters I am not competent to discuss, but it does seem clear that it is highly desirable to find better ways of providing us all with information about our individual and collective finances than we have at present. The obvious move is to introduce tighter legislation, backed by effective enforcement. But legalistic controls are both unduly rigid and costly to enforce. There is very often a fine line between an unacceptable gamble and a brilliant insight into the trend of the market or between a fraudulent misrepresentation of the prospects of a certain firm and recognition of its unappreciated potential. The law likes clear dichotomies. So in practice it often seems arbitrary and ineffectual, as well as unduly onerous and restrictive. There will be a need to prosecute and punish clearly criminal behaviour, but laws are never going to ensure the sound information a fair market requires.

I suggest, very tentatively, that there is a fairly simple first step towards a solution to this problem. Set up auditing services that are entirely independent of the institutions they audit, run by a suitable mix of ordinary people, accountants and economists. These services would be attractive to firms who were advantaged by having the truth about their performance be publicly available. These auditors would be employed not by firms but by a pubic foundation, which would assign teams of auditors to particular firms on a randomised roster. The firm would pay the foundation for its services. Such an audit could provide not only the sort of information and certification that traditional auditors provide but an assessment of the social and ecological sustainability of its activities. Such assessments involve much guessing and are inevitably fallible but they could supply a focus for public discussion that we lack at present in regard to many problems. In the case of near monopolies whose activities have substantial impacts on the community, submission to such audits might become compulsory if they were to meet public demand for accountability. It might even be possible to persuade the large accounting firms to convert some of their operations to this model.[1]

In general

In earlier drafts at this stage I included a rambling discussion of some problems of legal practice. I do believe that demarchic councils have other applications than the generation of sound

---

[1]   Since this chapter was written I have come across a very interesting book looking at developments in auditing from a different perspective than the one exemplified here: Jane Gleeson-White, *Six Capitals: the revolution capitalism has to have – or can accountants save the planet?* Sydney, Allen and Unwin, 2014.

policy. But discussing these possibilities sensibly is not possible in this sort of essay, and in any case distracts from the central focus on policy directed towards specific but pervasive problems of public goods and appropriate ways of reaching sound conclusions about what to do about them.

The specific examples I have discussed, climate change and international monetary policy affect everybody, even though doing anything about them involves very specific technical considerations. In this aspect they are untypical of most public goods, which are primarily good for a particular public with specific interests. Scientific knowledge is in principle a good for everybody, but many branches of science are accessible only to a few people with special skills and interests. Although the discoveries of the sciences are often of great practical importance and sustaining the process of investigation from which they emerge is expensive, the regulation of those activities and the disbursement of public funds to them must be left to those who are engaged in those enterprises. Calls to direct inquiry to serve other needs are generally futile. Scientific discoveries cannot be predicted. They are not there in the ground like mineral deposits waiting to be revealed by systematic search. They cannot be recognised like familiar ores. Appreciating their significance involves creative imagination of a very high order to grasp their significance in relation to existing problems in that field of inquiry. On the other hand scientists generally are not unaware of the social potential of what they are doing and pay attention to those considerations.

It is of fundamental importance that we respect the integrity of science as the pursuit of knowledge and also support the development of other areas of knowledge. The possibility of finding solutions to our problems is much more strongly dependent on the cognitive aspects of our culture and our willingness to use knowledge intelligently than on our having good intentions. Evil gets its opportunities from our stupid mistakes and our impatience. In the long run critical reason is very powerful, if only because every other means of attacking our problems inevitably fails to achieve what it sets out to do.

Equally inevitably our knowledge is often incapable of showing us how to achieve everything we feel we need to achieve. In the short run we must reconcile ourselves to that and do what we can to improve our knowledge. The basic thrust of demarchy is to decentralise those efforts so that what we try to do in any particular matter is as closely aligned as possible to specific problems in the light of the best understanding we can achieve of them. It is a call to stop looking at collective choices as implementing the will of the people and look at them as problems we need to understand and solve one by one.

Part Three

Objections Considered

In the following sections I have attempted not just to refute certain objections to my proposals, but also to amplify them. I want to enlarge the perspectives from which they may be seen to have advantages and to speculate about how they might be introduced in certain realistic scenarios. Whether they in fact deliver the results I claim they can must be established in practice, but they are unlikely to be tried in practice unless sufficient people are persuaded to put the necessary resources into the task. Inspiration is needed.

Objection 1: Is it worth it?

Perhaps the natural response to these arguments is: Are these issues worth all that fuss? Obviously we have to weigh costs and benefits when we embark on a substantial new investment of time and energy in the way I have been advocating. Equally obviously only trying it can provide a clear answer, but some preliminary objections need to be met. As I said at the beginning spontaneity is always attractive, but deliberate choice is often onerous.

The immediate objective of demarchy is to produce incremental improvements in how things are done in specific contexts where that is possible and desirable. Surely nobody seriously believes any longer that 'the old tried and true' ways of making decisions are unlikely to be improved. In every aspect of modern life the overall improvements we have achieved are largely due to incremental improvements, which have often come together to constitute historically significant advances in our forms of life. However, many of those process-es have been entirely unplanned. People and institutions have adapted to changes in their environment simply in making small changes in their habits. No organised process of choice has been necessary. In technology; this is undeniable. At some stage there is a clear innovation, like the invention of powered flight or radio transmission. But the effect of such innovations has depended on a continuous process of efforts to develop them that has been completely unregulated. At first they seemed of marginal significance in the context of existing demand. But these developments soon created new demands as they opened up new possibilities that got to be exploited without any organised collective response. Technologies demonstrate their value without any process of organised assessment.

Science by contrast, needs to assess new material as a con-tribution to knowledge. There is no simple practical test of that. The immediate practical applications of a proposal in science or scholarship are no guide to their value as knowledge. That can be assessed only by a complex and time-consuming process of constructing and assessing proposals for funding investigations and of peer review of their results in the context of existing knowledge. It may seem that my proposals are modelled more on science than on technology, and that that is a mistake. My answer is that it is indeed a mistake if it is taken as a proposal to apply such assessments to every attempt at deliberately influencing social change. Practicality is the supreme considera-tion. Most deliberate social change must continue to come from public discussions and other activities that have a direct influence on the behaviour of individuals and groups, quite independently of any formal process of assessment. In matters where these changes are generally accepted they will have a natural flow on to public policy through unorganised public debate. Up to the present we have relied in democratic countries on such informal social processes to cope with the problems of adapting our ways to changing conditions and opportunities, usually with good results. Many social practices have changed for the better. It is doubtful whether organised deliberation could have done better. It might well have done worse.

However, we now face many problems that demand strong collective action, where the consequences of failing to act are almost certainly going to be catastrophic. In at least some of these matters, such as climate change, it is of great importance that proposals for action be assessed very carefully as knowledge and not just in terms of short-term appeal. We need accurate knowledge of the factors involved and of the likely consequences of intervening in them. That seems indisputable. But more generally, where we are dealing with problems by legislation and administration in ways that interfere with normal social processes or involve setting up institutions that need to be financed by taxation, we cannot pretend to be relying on natural processes of adaptation to our environment. We have to take responsibility for our choices and make them on the best knowledge we can muster. Of course to a large extent the decision procedures I advocate are bits of social technology, as are many of our present political practices, and have to gain acceptance in much the same way as other technologies by proving themselves in practice, as well as in theory.

My first thinking about demarchy was motivated to a significant extent by the hope that it would constitute a process of collective self-education. Giving people a way of participating actively in decisions about matters that affected them directly in negotiation with others would encourage them to put themselves in other people's shoes, to attempt to find common ground and take a realistic approach to costs and benefits. At the same time they might, I hoped, see that there were better ways of dealing with problems than mobilising political blocs to wield power. More positively, demarchy might lead them to take pride and pleasure in the tangible public goods it produced and see their attachment to such goods not just in terms of the private benefits they derive from them, but in terms of the value they place on the network of communities with which they identify. There is a persistent assumption that community identification depends on geographical proximity. That is no longer the case. We can have close relations with people who share our interests all around the world.

Our present technology of mass voting is deficient and needs to be replaced where policy decisions are concerned. What I am proposing is introducing a new technology without displacing the old altogether. It is not a question of depriving people of their vote, but of adding a way of doing things that we see as needing to be done. Many people will want to hang on to the old ways, just as there is a nostalgic attachment to the monarchy. The British monarchy, for example, still has the last say on all legislation. No law is valid without the monarch's signature, but entrenched conventions ensure that this power is never exercised contrary to the decisions of parliament. What I am proposing can triumph not by suppressing its predecessor, but by setting its role in the context of a more comprehensive set of conventions. Demarchy seems capable of supplying the means of producing very important public goods in much more flexible and responsive ways and subjecting those ways to much closer examination. I think that there can be little doubt that if this is so it will create new demands for control of many social arrangements in the interest of those they purport to serve.

Clearly that will involve a much bigger investment of resources in decision-making. But that will not necessarily be mainly on the cost side of the ledger. It also creates opportunities for interesting and effective participation in significant social activities. Such activities are not everybody's cup of tea, but neither are most of the activities in which many people find participation rewarding. A major component of happiness for most people is to find things to do that they can do well and in which their achievements are accepted as significant at least among people who are interested in the same pursuits. Many of the activities we find satisfying are games of various kinds, in which the point of the activity is almost wholly internal to the game. It is not necessary that participating in the game be

accorded any substantial social significance for it to be mean-
ingful to the participants. But a culture in which people readily
find innocuous activities that prove satisfying to them is of
great social importance, a great common good. Some people
condemn the artificiality of so much of what modern culture
values. They hanker after simpler and more natural forms of
life that were possible only in very small communities, on a
limited scale. Such communities depended on unanimously
shared myths and practices. It is neither possible nor desirable
that we all attempt to return to that kind of social order, though
it may be important to our collective experience that some
attempt to do so. It is vital to our understanding of the limitations of our particular ways of living that we respect the
achievements of past communities and what they have
bequeathed to us.

The structured activities that people find satisfying and
challenging bind them to specialised communities, often on a
world scale. That in itself is an important good. If those
activities are also connected directly with the improvement of
some other important public good, that is a bonus. Football
may be good for the economy, but it deserves a place in our
public goods in its own right. A great deal of what we value is
our creation, and in no way to be devalued for not being
'natural'. Consider, for example science policy. Do we really
need to spend money that might be spent on relieving suffering
on astronomy? Of course, science does have unpredictable
benefits, but most scientific activity is directed at satisfying very
esoteric interests, which seem to proliferate exponentially with
diminishing returns, most of which are accessible only to the
initiated. We have to acknowledge the intrinsic value of science
as one of humanity's supreme achievements, but we do have to
balance its value against other values in allocating resources.

However, our most urgent and difficult problems arise out
of our interactions with natural necessities. This is particularly
the case where we are involved willy-nilly with the problems
of the use of irreplaceable resources. Our civilisation has been
built on the exploitation of cheap resources, priced at the cost of

extracting them plus a market-determined rent to their current owners, without any regard to future generations. That age is coming to an end. The prospect is that we will have to find ways of using the earth less destructively. Our present forms of governance tend to respond to such problems by issuing prohibitions, trying to control the clashes of interest between the private owners of natural resources and our collective long-term interest in preserving them and minimising the harmful effects of our present ways of using them.

While I think demarchic councils can improve our performance in such matters, I believe there are potentially better ways of handling such problems, but that doing so presupposes developments in our social technologies that at present we can only vaguely envisage. I have speculated about them in my earlier book, *Is Democracy Possible?*

There is an additional practical reason for employing citizen juries wherever important matters of political policy are involved, namely the growth of lobbyists and partisan think-tanks. These agencies deluge politicians and other influential figures with information and argument cleverly selected and presented for their audience to offer a seemingly overwhelming case for their specific interests. Public discussion, by contrast usually appears sporadic and confusing. We can counter that influence.

Objection 2: Liberty

The cost of demarchy that is of most concern to those who have come to value individual liberty as the supreme virtue of a polity is that it seems to invite a considerable increase in controls over what individuals are allowed to do. It is all very well to insist that it moves away from control by commands and prohibitions to more flexible and responsive controls. The fact remains that in one way or another it aims to replace a libertarian reliance on the responsibility and freedom of individuals to look after their own interests in the first place (the social problems that that produces are treated as residual or of secondary importance). Demarchy appears to be inherently paternalistic and socialising. It presupposes and encourages consensus and conformity that is at least constraining, if not repressive.

If one looks at the relative deprivations the libertarian ideology inflicts on the poor it is difficult to escape the conclusion that it is an ideology in the narrow Marxist sense, a myth that enables the rich to hide their exploitation of the poor. But the more interesting question is: Why do people who suffer under the myth buy it? Part of the answer is that what goods look most desirable in any culture are the things those who enjoy most prestige and power in that culture choose for themselves. Tell people that they can't have those things, but they can have something that is different but better, and they will suspect that you are trying to trick them, to sell them something they don't want. They prefer to listen to those who tell them that, with a little bit of luck, they too can have the same goodies the rich enjoy.

The other part of the answer is that the alternatives are depicted as worse than they in fact are. They are depicted in terms of their problems and failures. Any libertarian can expound the alleged failings of the British NHS, the corrupting effects of welfare dependency and the intrusiveness of regulators, ignoring constructive ways of dealing with such problems. A health fund or a school that caters only to people with a solid income automatically selects clients whose needs are more easily catered for than those of the disadvantaged. So it is very much easier for them to claim a higher success rate than an institution that covers the poor as well as the better off. Even so, private institutions are usually more expensive. To attract more skilled professionals they need to offer better pay and conditions. Education and health care are not only intrinsically labour-intensive. They also continually expand their demands as knowledge accumulates and diversifies.

There are very difficult problems in ensuring that a decent living is assured even to the losers in the competition to sell their labour on the market, just as there are systemic problems in the ways in which wealth grows more wealth at a much faster rate than the returns to labour. As long as the ability of people to provide the necessities of life for themselves is dependent on the market for their labour, it will be necessary to transfer wealth from the rich to the poor. Especially where technological change is constantly finding means of supplanting human work by machines and free trade brings the labour of less-developed societies into the market, competition for jobs will continue to depress the relative rewards to unskilled labour and leave a margin of unemployed people for whom there are no jobs. At the same time at the higher economic levels employers compete for the best labour, driving up its relative rewards. So far we have relied on the state to make the necessary redistribution. There is no possibility of changing that in the near future, just as there is little chance of displacing current bureaucratic procedures at this level, but alternatives may be possible in some matters.

Libertarians have postulated that the needs of the poor could be met by more enlightened and organised charity or philanthropy. In most of the great religions and in most moral traditions the rich have been told that helping the poor is not only an obligation but a privilege. Generosity is their distinctive virtue. That view of the matter is not dependent on any religious context. It is a matter of what we see as constituting success in life. Very few people would claim that the supreme achievement is to amass either money or power. What matters is what one does with them. Unfortunately it is too easy for the rich to claim that they are doing enough for the poor simply by paying their taxes and making the occasional donation to some worthy cause. In addition, the forms that charity took in more patriarchal societies involved treating people as dependents in ways that we now see as incompatible with their dignity. The poor resent any dependence on charity. I think there may be scope for collective projects that empower a group of poor people to control the resources made available to them by wealthy donors. An enlightened charity must recognise people's dignity and be prepared to support the needs of a community as that community, after due deliberation, sees them. If that community is encouraged to see a housing project as its own, not just a place where society dumps the losers, they will have a powerful incentive to see that it is well cared for and take pride in it. The quality of its public goods is the surest measure of the value that a society places on its collective identity. Perhaps the free choice in which the rich might find greatest satisfaction could be enlarging the range of what the poor can achieve when given the right kind of assistance.

Objection 3: Regulation

Our most important public goods are and will continue to be by-products of activities not explicitly designed to produce them. Our languages are the product of people striving to communicate with each other. A flourishing market is the product of innumerable particular exchanges. Our standards of conduct are the result of particular interactions between people. Each such field of interactions generates strong norms, of correct usage, of fair market prices and of acceptable behaviour. The most fundamental public good of any community is to be able to rely on mutually beneficial patterns of behaviour in all normal situations. Where the norms are generally respected, one can pursue nearly every activity one might desire freely, without fear of arbitrary interference. So the objection to excessive regulation is not just that it restricts individual freedom, but that it usurps the role of the normal processes of socialisation in ways that are self-defeating. Spontaneous cooperation is stifled by regimentation.

There are two major presuppositions of the processes of deliberate regulation. The negative one is the absence of intractable social conflicts. The positive one is confidence that where compulsion needs to be invoked to provide public goods it is seen as benign. It is often assumed that achieving the absence of sources of conflict is possible only in homogeneous, tightly closed communities. Such communities are no longer viable in our global order. What is now possible is for people to be members of many specialised communities each of which is homogeneous only in relation to its characteristic activities.

There are no total communities, but many communities of overlapping communities. It is true that in various ways such specialised communities may require more explicit regulation to achieve their objectives, which are often artefacts of our inventiveness, but that regulation must, as far as possible, arise from discussion among those involved in their activities and not be treated as mere means towards other ends. Racism, sexism and religious intolerance are not only unjust to many individuals, but they preclude the full realisation of many goods that can only reach their full potential if they operate on the basis of their own needs, unrestricted by irrelevant considerations. Avoiding sexism does not mean ignoring differences of gender altogether, but being clear about where they are relevant. We can get beyond national chauvinism without pretending that there are no such things by looking at our problems in a global perspective. Very many of our activities involve interactions within a diversity of frameworks of interaction that transcend national boundaries. They cannot be regulated satisfactorily by individual countries, but they cannot exist without appropriate regulation and we cannot flourish to our full potential without them. The internet cannot exist without a recognised authority to license URLs.

We can have confidence in compulsion being benign to the extent that we are satisfied that it is kept to the minimum necessary for its particular purpose. The effect of attempts to enforce norms unnecessarily is often to turn what were free public goods to which we can all contribute and in which we can all rejoice into the property of the guardians, something onerous, sterile and oppressive to many people. The enforcers see themselves as having a special appreciation of the true nature and importance of those goods that is lacking in those who would subvert them. Where there is the question of deliberate organisation to supply public goods in such fields as education, health care and public facilities I have already offered my suggestions about how to involve the consumers in influencing the supply. There are, however other matters where the central problems can be dealt with only on a much larger scale, and where regulation has to be more paternalistic, such as matters of public hygiene, safety regulations and the exploitation of non-renewable resources. Even in such cases it seems preferable to entrust supervision of the relevant authorities to suitably representative councils rather than to the attempts of politicians to interpret what people are prepared to vote for.

I remarked earlier that many public goods consist in protecting us from various dangers where we cannot do so as individuals. Those who react against such regulation dismiss the 'nanny state' or intrusive busybodies, but the costs of neglecting such regulations are exhibited with tragic regularity. Modern science has produced many effective but dangerous medications. There is general acceptance of their availability being limited, under professional control. We have adopted a different approach to 'recreational' drugs. They are attractive but harmful and have no therapeutic value. So we ban them altogether, ineffectually and at great cost. Fashion, curiosity and the desire to escape from the real world create a demand that is perpetuated by addiction, in spite of the inevitable disillusionment. The demand is supplied by highly organised and immensely profitable crime syndicates that overtax and often corrupt law enforcement agencies, and spill over into other crimes, theft to finance expensive addiction, violence and even murder. The war on drugs blames the problem on the suppliers, but the real problem is the demand side.

There are better ways of dealing with the problem. Recreational drugs could be available at a reasonable price in small quantities from qualified and registered drug counsellors to people who register as users, with strict controls over using multiple identities. Counsellors would need to be satisfied that the user was well aware of the dangers and that addicts were given every inducement to seek a cure, but the ultimate responsibility for using the drug would lie with the user. Such a scheme would be paternalistic, but realistic and relatively easily policed. It could take the supply of drugs out of its criminal and anti-social context, even if it did not succeed in pricing all illegal suppliers out of the market. There undoubtedly would always be a significant number of drug addicts in the community, but that the problem would be the user's problem rather than the community's. The professionals charged with running such programs might be supervised by former addicts.

One of the basic obstacles to introducing such a scheme lies in the dynamics of populist democracy. For some it is the role of the state to stand up for what is right and wage war on what is evil. For them the only conceivable approach to the drug problem is total prohibition, rigorously enforced. Even those who don't share this rigidly moralistic approach are fearful of creating a situation in which drug use is not only legitimised but made too easy. So the electoral consequences of a politician advocating anything short of criminalising drug use are almost certainly fatal. On the other hand, I'm very inclined to think that a council composed of those with expertise and experience in the matter and a sample of ordinary people would decide on something of the sort I have suggested and that it could undercut the drug trade.

The primary role of regulation in most matters where potentially dangerous activities are involved must be to ensure that there is coordination about standard practices of eliminating danger. Standardisation enables regulations to be well understood and normally taken for granted. Such regulations will often appear irrelevant in some cases, but it is necessary to deter the imprudent from cutting corners in ways that may have dangerous consequences for others. That is the downside of living in a diverse but interrelated technological and social configuration. The best we can do is to ensure that in each particular case the regulatory regime combines effectiveness with ease of compliance. The right balance between these considerations is most likely to be struck by discussions between those who are involved in production and the consumers they serve.

Objection 4: Economy

Any advocate of the organised production of public goods has to confront the economist's argument that such goods are almost always over or under supplied. I have already criticised the assumption that the money people are prepared to spend on an item is a sound measure of the value they place on it. A person's not having to pay for a good does not automatically lead to their undervaluing it. A lot depends on whether they are proud of it and identify with it or see it as imposed on them. It is likely that people use a public service more frequently if it is free than if they had to pay for each use. That is not always a bad thing. In 2014 the Australian government was convinced that we go to the doctor too frequently. So they propose to introduce a small co-payment to deter us from doing so fecklessly. In the face of public protests this proposal was withdrawn. There are certainly advantages in people keeping in regular contact with their medical advisor, even if not every visit is strictly necessary. Perhaps they should be encouraged to do so. The cost is small and the dangers of deterring those who most need regular medical attention are serious.

When it comes to private consumption goods few of us buy only to meet necessities. We buy bigger, faster and more lavishly equipped cars, most of whose capacities we never use, waste a quarter of the food we buy, and clothe ourselves for style rather than function. This relatively extravagant expenditure enables us to use these things as expressions of our self-image.

Similarly, in regard to many public goods a little extravagance expresses our communal self-image. That is no small part of life for us both individually and collectively. To be human is to want to go beyond mere functionality. The New Year's Eve fireworks matter a lot to many people as an expression of communal identity. That is difficult to fit into cost–benefit analyses.

It looks easy enough to do a cost–benefit analysis on the NYE fireworks. Suppose the cost is two million dollars and that two million people turn out to view them. It is reasonable to assume that they would be on average prepared to pay a dollar a head for the spectacle. But what about the externalities, the cost of the clean up afterwards, the annoyance to those who hate the noise and disturbance of their neighbourhood? Perhaps we can price these as well. What if they come to another two million dollars? That is still only two dollars a head. But what about the opportunity costs? Two million dollars could do a lot for the homeless or many other worthy causes. We cannot cover them all. Ultimately, it misses the point of the shared experience.

The intractable problem is the budget. We do not like having to pay for services that we use much less frequently than others. Most of us are quite sure that we could make better use of the money we contribute to public funds than the present dispensers of those funds. That is not just the result of egocentricity or of refusal to acknowledge one's debts to one's community. It affects all insurance schemes. One pays for those who neglect their health, for those who are careless of their own property or run unnecessary risks. It rarely pays to take out insurance if one can accept the risks it covers. There is no point in paying others to take the risk on themselves. If we regard taxation as just paying for insurance the better off must see it as a poor deal, imposed on them by bad politics.

It is easy to fall into the fallacy of treating public expenditure as a dead loss. The problem is to produce public goods that may give more satisfaction to people than the private goods that they might buy with the money. That is not necessarily a matter of putting the good of others before one's own. Rather it is a matter of an expansive view of one's identity. A narrowly selfish attitude deprives everybody, including its protagonists, of much of what makes life worth living. It is superficial and self-destructive. Much of the fulfilment people can find in life derives from the various communities with which they identify. They enjoy the collective possessions and achievements that they regard as their own. Their traditions and heritage, the functioning of their institutions, the triumphs of their endeavours, are things that command admiration and unite them in rejoicing. The real difficulty is that it is impossible to identify with what one resents as an imposition, as the product of a poor political system and a defective bureaucracy. On the other hand, if the achievements of an instrumentality are seen as the product of a sound and transparent decision-process that brings important benefits to people who appreciate them, it becomes easy to take pride in contributing to them, even if one gets no other benefit from them oneself.

If a particular complex of decisions is seen as supplying important elements in the functioning of our social ecosystem, we are inclined to accept it in its concrete form, as a single living thing, just as we appreciate a landscape, a garden or any arrangement of diverse elements that achieves a certain aesthetic or functional unity. Each such functioning whole is unique in its way, but by no means the only satisfactory possibility or the best conceivable arrangement. Conservatives rightly emphasise that we need to accept existing traditional arrangements in many areas on this kind of basis. Politics is not just economics or morals or power, it is also aesthetics. These distinct and often conflicting dimensions are interdependent in complex ways. They admit of various choices, and how those choices are made matters a great deal to the satisfaction we can take in their results.

In a very complex social ecosystem, there is only one way of arriving at an acceptable overall result, namely to make each of the component arrangements as good as possible in terms of the needs it serves, and to provide constructive means of coordinating them where necessary. There is no single purpose that the components of an ecosystem serve. Each adapts in its own way to the environment in which it grows and reproduces itself. Out of that process there grows a certain integrated order of interdependence. There can be no guarantee that this approach will work in every context, much less that it is capable of solving all our problems, but I think we must push it as far as we possibly can. At the level of particular organisms we have to assist them to survive with a view both to their autonomy and their services to other organisms. At the level of complex ecosystems we need to identify and deal with threats to their stability, even as we intervene to develop them to suit our purposes. What we cannot do is assume that we will be able to survive any change that may happen in our ecosystem, including those caused by our uncontrolled exploitation of it. The risks of that approach are unacceptable.

Objection 5: Conflicting advice?

There seems to be a contradiction in the approach I am taking to public goods. On the one hand I insist on the importance of specific public goods and the importance of cooperation between the various stakeholders in a particular area of policy to get the best result for all their interests in that particular area, while on the other hand I seem anxious to deny any specific interests to the larger organisms in which the smaller are involved. It looks as if I were saying that the functioning of any whole is merely a matter of the functioning of its parts. Or in terms of value that the whole has no value except in so far as it serves the interests of its components. In ecological terms, the ecosystem is important only insofar as it supports the organisms that go to make it up. The answer is that particular organisms have value both in themselves and in the functions they perform for other organisms. The whole has a certain value in itself, but, as far as we can see no function in some broader context.

In political terms, both extremes, individualism and collectivism, are absurd. Even more importantly, neither the functioning nor the value of the part can be reduced to the role it has in just one particular whole. Each cell and each animal has its own agenda and many other roles that arise out of their interactions with other organisms. Think of bees and all the different interconnections they have with other organisms. On the other hand, so do each of the larger configurations which those cells or animals go to constitute. In nature every complex entity relates to all other complex entities in virtue of properties that it derives from the particular way its components are organised. This is as much the case in chemistry as in biology or sociology. At the macro level H_2O in the form of ice interacts with other solids in familiar patterns of interactions between solids. At the micro level the molecules of H_2O are interacting with such factors as radiation in quite different patterns. Those micro level interactions, however, affect whether the ice melts or stays frozen. Similarly, teams of people organised in certain patterns interact with other teams in ways that individuals cannot. Those people continue to have their own agendas and interact within the organisation and with their other connections while performing their role in the group. The stability of the group depends on the compatibility of the various other things its members are doing with their role in the group. In nature what complexes come to be formed and continue to survive is a matter of chance. All complexes depend on combinations of circumstances that are not guided by any purpose or superior force. In social activities we construct various wholes by persuading other people to serve its needs as well as by using knowledge of natural processes to manipulate animals, vegetables and minerals to produce the results we want.

I have sought to emphasise the dangers of top-down organisation, particularly because of its tendency to treat the people it organises as mere parts of a machine in the interests of a certain sort of efficiency and predictability. I have also been anxious to reject the tendency to value people only insofar as they contribute to the sum total of value. But I do not want to deny that top-down organisation is indispensible in some connections, especially in activities directed to producing specific results. Policies do need to be compatible with each other as well as efficient as a means to a particular end. But I want to emphasise that it is also appropriate in deciding what sort of results we want. At the same time I want to emphasise that we seek satisfaction in well-organised activities with which we identify as part of our multi-dimensional selves. Each person is attracted by many different possibilities, not all of which can be realised at the same time or even sequentially. One has to decide which to pursue and how much attention to devote to each in the context of one's basic needs, but beyond that in view of our sense of what we want to be. Often those choices are the result of chance encounters and discoveries rather than deliberate planning. Similarly, various social groups engage in specific activities that individuals cannot attain on their own, but in which they can gain satisfaction.

It is not possible for individuals to explore all possibilities open to them, but it is most desirable in the case of both individual and collective choices to have a variety of possibilities among which to choose relatively independently, leaving room for invention and experimentation. In this respect the value of demarchy is that it offers people many roles that they can perform if they find them attractive. In that context they can get enhanced satisfaction from the success of the complex to which they are contributing. All sports and hobbies present a challenge to those who participate in them to do something that is difficult to do well, even though that serves no higher purpose. My hope is that demarchic councils would be attractive to many people just because they present an opportunity to perform well in a difficult role, as well as serving an important purpose. The social value of such motivations is not something one can put a price on. Authoritarian polities treat all their members as needing to be kept in order. A free society depends on getting them to want to do what needs to be done without the need for carrots and sticks. It can be more economical.

The fatal flaw of democratic centralism as conceived by the Bolsheviks was to neglect this need for flexibility. The soviet councils, the productive teams at grass roots, were supposed to discuss all the issues that affected them and arrive at a common view on them. At the next higher level the views of the various soviets were to be discussed and reconciled, until unanimity was achieved at the highest level. That enabled the planners to prescribe the allocation of resources to specific objectives. These allocations were in turn given more specific form in terms of resources and objectives at each level, back down to the soviets, who would enthusiastically set to meet their objectives prescribes to them, confident that the whole was being organised for the best. It could not and did not work. Too many people were required to perform impossible tasks. The resources assigned to them were too often inadequate to the tasks assigned to them. So they faked compliance. The specific needs of real people were lost in ever more abstract objectives.

Objection 7: Externalities

It may seem that the great danger in giving primacy to the specific in decision-making is that it neglects externalities. An externality is a result of market-related actions that have good or bad effects for which the producer is neither rewarded nor penalised by the market. The market doesn't charge a polluter for the toxic effluents it sends into the atmosphere nor reward a discoverer for producing knowledge that everybody can use. Firms that produce externalities do so, not because they are keen to do so, but for other reasons. So we try other incentives to encourage producers to do things that produce desirable externalities and discourage actions that produce undesirable ones. It might seem that one of the main tasks of government is to find and deploy such means as will ensure those desirable results are obtained. If policy is narrowly focussed on the direct results of an activity, even on a specific public good, it will tend to neglect externalities just as surely as the market does. But we need to tread very cautiously.

Back in the 1960s a group of Hungarian scholars to whom I am deeply indebted produced a deep analysis of what was wrong with socialism as it was understood in Eastern Europe. It was Australia's good fortune that several of them spent most of their exile here. One of the problems that they identified in the system was that it 'internalised all externalities'. Whatever undesirable consequence attended any policy had to be dealt with within the system. That soon leads to stasis. Changing anything becomes too difficult. It is a fairly obvious conse-quence of attempting to control everything, but it also has a moral aspect. Fairness seems to demand that when actions of others impose disadvantages on a person those others ought to compensate her. In an ideally just world nobody would be worse off as a result of actions over which they had no control. In the real world we have to take our chances with the effects of a large range of events that affect our fortunes.

In a market economy we do not hold an entrepreneur responsible for the losses her entry into the market inflicts on her competitors. We allow bankrupts to terminate their liabilities to their creditors. More generally, we take action to penalise producers of externalities only in certain cases where the consequences are systematically important and avoidable. In some cases this is simple enough. It is not only unfair to particular people, but also damaging to the ecosystem, when producers can discharge the toxic waste of their production process into the environment. Fortunately, it is usually easy to detect and penalise such actions. Unfortunately, it may mean that a plant has to be shut down, putting many workers out of a job, and the only things that can be done about that are just to relieve their pain. What we can or ought to do in particular cases for people who are severely affected by events outside their control is often a difficult decision involving many conflicting considerations, especially when it takes the form of international movements of millions of refugees. Such problems call for international action based on a sober discussion of the moral, economic and social dimensions of the crisis. Unfortunately, populist democracy with a national focus rarely produces such discussion. The issues are oversimplified and the perspective narrowed. We must use better ways of arriving at decisions on such matters.

Many positive externalities are valuable public goods, as an articulate and well-educated community emerges from individuals pursuing an education for their own reasons. So, just as we attempt to restrict activities that have negative externalities, we attempt to encourage activities that have positive ones. But there is a danger in making decisions about specific goods on the grounds of their being likely to have particular externalities. That perspective leads to such goods as education and health being treated as mere means to other objectives, especially financial ones, in a purely mechanical way. On the one hand, the goods themselves need to have, and to be seen to have, value in their own right. They are constituents of a good life and not mere means to other ends. Reducing education to vocational training is destructive. On the other hand, the factors involved in producing the desired externalities are normally quite complex—the desired results are not assured and their value as means is insecure, while their intrinsic value is discounted. Once again the analogy of the ecosystem is very relevant. The primary factor in the health of the whole is the health of each component in terms of its own needs.

If I am right, while the specific authorities dealing with particular problems in some matter of health care or education should be aware of the positive and negative externalities their decisions may produce, and minimise or maximise them in suitable ways, their primary focus should be to optimise the particular good they deal with. There is a danger, very often displayed in present politics, of concentrating on certain economic objectives, because they are so obvious and uncontroversial, and treating the particular services that may produce them as if they were just means to those particular ends. That leads very often, I think, to actions that do not respect the needs of the activities so treated. That in turn brings failure and disillusion. We get programmes that treat education simply as a means of increasing the supply of certain kinds of skills, instead of encouraging people to be interested in developing their potential. An ampler education allows finding work that is interesting and important. On the broader scale it creates a community that is inventive and opens up wider horizons. Don't manipulate people or treat them as mere means if you want them to contribute creatively to their society.

Most of the desirable characteristics we want our societies to exhibit are externalities that cannot be produced by direct action, especially by legislation. They are the result of many different factors conspiring to produce them. It is a characteristic failing of top-down planning and of populist politics to imagine that there is always a way of producing a desired result by determined action directed at penalising undesirable behaviour. That is almost invariably ineffectual. To take a familiar example, if you want people to behave well at a sporting event pay attention to removing causes of friction. Provide comfortable individual seating. Make it possible for them to book a seat or to be assured that there is a fair system of allocating seating, and so on. Make it easy for people to act agreeably and they are very likely to do so because they enjoy the mutual recognition it brings them. Demarchy rests on the fundamental assumption that a society where things are well organised to meet the requirements of its members naturally generates practices of civility and constructive initiative.

Recognising what specific considerations are relevant to a problem is rarely easy or obvious. There can be no simple prescription for hitting the right level of description for understanding what we are doing. Just as the same action may be described as ' just pressing a bit of metal' through a variety of contextual frames to 'setting off WWI', so there is no uniquely right description of any psychological or social activity, even in relation to a specific type of context. On the other hand, there are always plenty of descriptions that, although right in some contexts, in others are simply wrong. In some contexts all we need know is that this stuff is H_2O. In others it is vital to know whether it is ice or steam. Populist democracy is too easily focused on relieving symptoms rather than curing the disease.

Even if you, the reader, accept most of what I have said, you may well be left with a feeling that it all fails to come to grips with the most urgent political problems of our world. Thousands of people are being slaughtered, millions forced into desperate misery. Just what are we supposed to do about Syria, Iraq or Afghanistan, or about the conflicts over jurisdiction in the South China Sea, or Ukraine? There is no possibility that the main parties to such conflicts are going to take the slightest notice of any demarchic council. At most such advice may put some pressure on the powers involved to come to the negotiating table. Diplomacy of a very traditional kind, based on power-trading, does sometimes work. In the long run, however, the only solution to such problems is to cut down the pretentions of states and ideological interests to call on every possible resource to assert what they see as their rights. The only long-term solution is to cut down the role of power—especially of threatening damage—in human affairs, by developing sensible practices of collective decision-making.

Conclusion

Radical thinking about political questions has been dominated by economic theory for almost two hundred years. F.A. Hayek and Karl Marx explore the extremes of economic and social thinking. Hayek's hypothesis is that almost all human inter-actions can be seen as exchanges of things of equal value in the market. That secures the sovereignty of the consumer, to the maximum benefit of all. The role of government is simply to ensure the conditions that make a fair market possible. Marx's view is that the market in the means of production must be abolished. It gives sovereignty to producers. The producers force labour to sell itself to those who have capital for less than the value of what it produces. So the capitalists inevitably become richer than those who do not have capital. Since it is not possible to ensure that everybody owns much the same capital, the only solution is to abolish market exchange as the basic mechanism for organising production. The ultimate objective of communism is a regime of cooperative relations between producers and consumers. In the interim a transitional period of state socialism is necessary to strip the capitalists of their capital goods and rearrange production.

The Social Democrat response to these extremes has been twofold: First, to guarantee a decent return to labour by restraining competition for jobs that lowers the price of labour — the price of labour being set collectively through trade unions or by legislation. Second, to use progressive taxation to pay for free services that provide a decent life for those who have nothing to sell that the market will buy. In the middle of the twentieth century all democratic regimes adopted this solution to some extent. In many ways it was amazingly successful. It supplied almost all citizens of well-managed countries with a high standard of living and unprecedented social and personal security.

Even at the height of the successes of social democracy, Hayek rejected it, offering many perceptive criticisms of its operating procedures. He always insisted that he shared the humanist values that led many people to support social democracy, but saw irremediable flaws in its procedures. He hit on the word 'demarchy' to give a name to this view. His own alternative proposals involved constitutional changes designed to ensure that only fully mature and responsible people could exercise state power. Hayek hardly addressed the problems of decision procedures and so failed to come to grips with the basic problems of the democracy he rejected. In any case his proposals had no chance of winning much support. They harked back to classical nineteenth century liberalism, ignoring the nature of the changes since then. However, as the shine wore off the welfare state, his criticisms of it got more attention.

The weaknesses of social democracy were twofold: First, the procedures by which the state produced and implemented its decisions were seen as dangerous, inefficient and often ineffectual in meeting the requirements of its citizens, and second that it was hampered by its national focus from addressing global problems of all sorts and especially reaping the benefits of international free trade. It was seen as parasitic on the market. The fans of the market insisted that unleashing its power would cause a great surge in overall wealth, and that on that rising tide 'all boats would rise.' That didn't happen. The increase of wealth went almost entirely to the richest one per cent.

At present there are no plausible suggestions about how to reverse the processes of capitalism, but there are ways, I claim, of remedying the basic flaws in democracy as we have it and so making better decisions about both social welfare and global problems. I offer practical proposals based on procedures that can easily be implemented if enough people are prepared to put in the required work and resources. The success of those proposals in practice probably depends on enough of the one per cent being prepared to use their wealth to support the widespread experimentation with better ways of reaching collective decisions without any return to themselves except the satisfactions of having done something worthwhile and being recognised as having done that.

It is most unlikely that there will be any mass conversion to the views I have outlined. They would first need to be tested and prove useful in practice on a scale sufficiently large to command attention. In a modern society that needs organisation and bold initiatives. Competent and dedicated people will need to devote persistent attention to identifying instances where the introduction of a demarchic council is likely to succeed in solving existing problems. They will need to make well-designed proposals for the scope of the council, and the formulae of sortition (random selection). They will need to stimulate communications between the council and the people it aims to serve. The representatives may need to be compensated for their efforts and expert advice paid for.

There is a history, going back to antiquity, of the wealthy wanting to display their munificence and social awareness by establishing independent foundations to support important public goods. It may well be that my proposals will appeal to some such people as offering a middle way between adversarial democracy and a market that is incapable of meeting the need for public goods. Such initiatives would provide a focus for wider public interest, transcending current political ideologies. Should it prove possible to get the movement in favour of demarchy rolling, opinion in its favour might develop quite rapidly. Discontent with adversarial politics is not likely to diminish. My proposals have the great advantage that if they are tried and fail, nothing will be lost if we learn from that failure.

Of course, these are just hopes. Abandoning the nationalist viewpoint would take a lot of the grandeur and excitement out of politics. People are reluctant to abandon their illusions, which have so often been part of what gives meaning to their lives. In my youth we sang with uncritical enthusiasm *Land of Hope and Glory*, that extraordinary hymn to blatant imperialism. Now it can only be sung with a certain irony. Retaining the relics of old institutions is not just sentimentality. They are part of the narratives that constitute our identities and enshrine our origins. But our progeny will expect more of us than merely handing on the memory of the past. We have the capacity to set up the context with which they will have to cope. Most of our capacities we owe to our ancestors. We can repay them only by adding to the heritage they left to us.

Finally, it may seem that demarchy is based on pedestrian considerations, leaving little room for more ambitious values, especially those associated with grand visions of human destiny. It certainly makes no pretention to the sort of cosmic or transcendent significance that has inspired so many religious and political movements. But it is not just a matter of pragmatic experimentation. It is deeply morally serious. It offers people roles in which they can express what is best about their capacity for creative cooperation. In that way it is a realistic and sober way of giving power to the people in the light of both our unprecedented problems and our novel capacities for understanding them.

That demarchy will succeed inevitably seems very improbable. But in history, as in biological evolution, only the antecedently improbable ever happens. If demarchy is to come alive, it needs to be incarnated in images, dramatic events, rituals and sensibilities. All I can give it is a name.

Appendix 1

Demarchy, Deliberative Polling and other developments

There are close affinities in outlook between demarchy and deliberative democracy,[1] which is a long established movement that has enjoyed widespread approval. The essential difference is that deliberative polling committees are purely consultative and assembled episodically. Demarchy looks to its councils as having more authority and in many cases a more permanent status, with a regular turnover of membership. Demarchy is a long-term movement towards changing the accepted practices of determining public policy. Deliberative democracy is a matter of improving, rather than questioning existing procedures. Its work is typically commissioned by governments seeking to legitimise their policies by thorough consultation. My hope is that as people become more aware of the limitations of deliberative polling they will move towards demarchy.

The main limitations of deliberative polling spring from the fact that the group involved in coming to a decision on the matter referred to it does not bear any ongoing institutional

---

[1]   See the Stanford University website (cdd.stanford.edu) which gives a survey of deliberative polling around the world, particularly as organised by Professor James Fishkin. In Australia, see the New Democracy website.

identity or responsibility for its decision. So its recommendations are easily dismissed if they do not suit the strategies of the politicians. The questions assigned to a deliberative poll are usually framed by the politicians (or other authorities) who commission the poll. That problem is exacerbated by the fact that the matters referred to such committees are often broad policy questions, rather than the specific problems I want them to tackle. Above all, I believe that the initiative must come from the wider community if it is to constitute a remedy for our present ills. Demarchy wants the public to tell the politicians what it wants and demand that they deliver it.

One of the few cases where a deliberative body has been given a prior commitment that its decisions would be implemented occurred in China in 2005. Under the direction of Professor Fishkin of Stanford University, the Deliberative Polling® project in Zeguo township, Wenling City, allowed a scientific sample of ordinary citizens to deliberate about which infrastructure projects would be funded in the coming year. The resulting decisions were accepted and implemented by the ruling party officials. It was considered a success, and widely applauded in China and internationally.

Clearly, if the ruling group in China is serious about responding to aspirations for more democracy without introducing multiple parties, and also suppressing corruption, demarchy is a very attractive proposal. That it has not pushed in this direction seems to be related to the role of the party apparatus in managing the huge changes taking place in China. The relatively smooth transitions that have occurred have been managed by local party officials using a range of carrots and sticks to reconcile people to massive dislocations. Clearly if the people affected had had more say in the process, change would have been much slower. Inevitably the wide discretion that officials have enjoyed has led to a great deal of corruption at all levels of the party as the price of its success. As the pace of change slows and more carrots go to corrupt officials, that situation may change quite rapidly.

Many ideas in recent thinking converge to some degree with the position I have outlined. A very useful discussion of experience in public deliberation is Lyn Carson *et al* (eds) *The Australian Citizens' Parliament and the Future of Deliberative Democracy*, University Park PA, Pennsylvania State University Press, 2013. An older but still useful book is *The Deliberative Democracy Handbook* edited by J. Gastil and P. Levine, San Francisco, Jossey-Bass, 2005. The work of Archon Fung and others on 'mini publics', for example, is important in its attention to the problem of matching authorities to the real connections between diverse interests and breaking away from traditional assumptions of sovereignty.

Of course that leaves enormous problems, such as the population problem and capitalism itself, quite untouched. If we work at dealing with the defects we can remedy we may well gain insight into other factors that remain unrecognised at present.

Constitutions and conventions

My proposals envisage change in the roles of political structures and procedures by convention rather than by legal
enactments. I have referred to the British constitution, which
rests entirely on conventions,[1] to show how even very radical
changes can come about in this way. Most people are not likely
to seen that as very convincing. The British case is usually seen
as the product of an idiosyncratic culture and the common law
tradition, dominated by precedent. The British constitution
grew out of a series of historical circumstances that are unlikely
to be repeated. No doubt that is correct.

However, the contrast between written constitutions and
convention is very misleading. How strongly people consider
themselves bound by decisions taken by their ancestors is a
matter of current conventions. Constitutions can be changed.
Even when certain provisions remain unchanged, they are
subject to changing interpretations. They cannot possibly
envisage relevant social developments and the unprecedented
problems they pose. Even carefully constructed constitutions
often fail to recognise important political institutions that they
take for granted. For example, cabinet government is an

---

[1] 'Convention', that is, in the sense of generally accepted standards or
customs as opposed to the constitutional conventions (meetings of dele-
gates) that took place in Philadelphia in 1787 and Paris from 1792-1795.

important part of the regulation of power in the Westminster tradition, but the Australian constitution, among others, fails to mention it. The fundamental aspect of the matter is that constitutions require interpretation, which is entirely a matter of convention.

The resemblance between interpreting constitutions and interpreting sacred texts has often been noted. On the one hand fundamentalists pick on texts that support their views when read in the light of certain doctrinal assumptions and produce ingenious interpretations to explain away less supportive texts. They find definitive answers to contemporary questions by ignoring literary form, historical change and other ways of framing the issues. On the other hand, liberal theologians insist on differences of context, the need for coherence, and the complexity of the issues, thus undercutting any decisive force attached to a particular formula. They are accused of supplanting the sacred text with wishful thinking. Whichever view one adopts, the answer to most contemporary issues is inevitably to some extent arbitrary. Sacred texts are not an adequate guide in practice. Nor are written constitutions.

It remains true that as long as a power is attached to an office, it is likely that holders of the office will be tempted to ignore conventions about the proper exercise of the office. In the Westminster tradition the monarch appoints the ministers who are responsible for government and can dismiss them. The convention that has been observed by British monarchs for two centuries is that a government may not be dismissed as long as it enjoys the support of a majority in the lower house of parliament. In Australia state governors and Commonwealth governors-general are nominally appointed by the British monarch on the advice of the government and exercise the monarch's powers on her or his behalf. Their role is largely ceremonial.

Nevertheless, in 1932 the then governor of New South Wales dismissed the state government, which was still supported by the lower house, on the pretext that it had committed a crime, although it had not been found guilty by any court of law. In 1975 the then governor-general dismissed the elected government on the ground that, in his judgment, it no longer had the money with which to govern. In both cases the governor called an election in contravention of the normal prerogative of the government to choose the date of an election before its term of office expires. In both cases they got away with it. The electors chose not to reinstate the dismissed governments, which, whatever their merits, were disadvantaged by the slur cast on their administration.

What counts in the long run is whether public opinion insists on upholding convention. Of course, the same applies to written law. But it is essential that in addition to texts there be clear conventions and that both be respected.